CREATING WITH POLYMER CLAY

DESIGNS,
TECHNIQUES
& PROJECTS

STEVEN FORD & LESLIE DIERKS

Lark Books

Published by Lark Books
50 College Street
Asheville, North Carolina, U.S.A., 28801

© 1996 by Steven Ford and Lark Books

Art Director: Kathleen Holmes
Photography: Richard Babb
Illustrations: Orrin Lundgren
Production: Elaine Thompson, Kathleen Holmes

Library of Congress Cataloging in Publication Data
Ford, Steven, 1964–
    Creating with polymer clay : designs, techniques,
& projects / Steven Ford and Leslie Dierks.
        p.   cm.
    Includes bibliographical references and index.
    ISBN 0-937274-95-X
    1. Plastics craft.   I. Dierks, Leslie.   II. Title.
TT297.F7   1996   95-21974
745.572--dc20   CIP

10 9 8 7 6 5 4 3 2

Printed in Hong Kong

ISBN 0-937274-95-X

PREVIOUS PAGE: VESSEL BY KATHLEEN DUSTIN.
THIS AND OPPOSITE PAGES: CLOCK BY PIERRETTE BROWN
ASHCROFT, PLATTER BY ANGIE WIGGINS, VESSELS BY STEVEN
FORD, BIRD HOUSE BY BRIDGET ALBANO.

CONTENTS

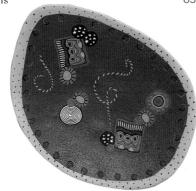

A COLLECTION OF BUTTERFLIES, STEVEN FORD AND DAVID FORLANO, AVERAGE SIZE APPROX. 2-1/2" X 2" (6.5 X 5 CM)

 ompared to the craft materials that artisans have used for generations, polymer clay is a real newcomer. It was invented amid the scientific frenzy during the mid-20th century that witnessed the birth of an entire family of plastic materials. Initially polymer clay was used primarily for making dolls, puppets, and miniature figures, and some forms of the material became very popular among school children during the 1960s.

Within the last decade the craft potential of this material has been "discovered." The individual artists who first started experimenting with it found that polymer clay was a good substitute for other materials that required specialized equipment or extensive training. Mainly through trial and error, and often by accident, they discovered its remarkable versatility. Soon the word spread, and today there are individuals all over the world comparing polymer clay techniques via the Internet. Others share ideas through local chapters of a national guild devoted solely to the promotion of this material.

Why are so many so excited? This material can be modeled, molded, carved, woven, and treated just about any other way you can imagine. Its full range of brilliant colors can be mixed to achieve the most subtle effects or the most vibrant. It is clean, neat, and easily stored away, and it doesn't shrink, fade, or dry out. Polymer clay requires no special training and no exotic tools or equipment. Best of all, its possibilities are practically unlimited; you can use it to make jewelry, bowls, frames, lamps, holiday decorations, buttons, games, boxes, and just about anything else.

Because it is such a new material, the full capabilities of polymer clay are still evolving. This book includes the designs of many of the finest contemporary artists working in this medium, but this is just the beginning. Let their ideas and techniques inspire you to take the next step. Discover your own new and exciting ways to create beautiful objects from polymer clay.

Because of polymer clay's wide-ranging capabilities and its relatively recent origin, many artists have turned to a variety of long-established craft traditions for precedents. Some striking examples of contemporary polymer clay work show strong influences from such crafts as glass caning, glass lampwork, micromosaics, stone inlay, carved bone and ivory, ceramic tile, mokume-gane metalwork, and ikat textiles, among others.

Of all the traditional techniques currently being applied to polymer clay, probably the most familiar is canework. Caning is a glass technique for creating intricate cross-sectional designs. The most well-known examples of this technique are the Venetian glass paperweights constructed in the style called *millefiori*, which literally means a thousand flowers.

MILLEFIORI CANEWORK DISK AND BEADS, DONNA KATO

As with glass, polymer clay caning starts with rods or slabs of material in various colors that are assembled in a large block to form a pattern. The block is then stretched out to reduce the scale of the cross-sectional image. The long block, or cane, can be cut and reassembled to repeat the image in a more complex design, then stretched out again to further reduce its scale.

Using a combination of opaque and translucent polymer clays, Donna Kato successfully imitates the unique look of fused *millefiori* glass. In glass, this technique can be done only with specialized kilns, grinding equipment, and polishing wheels. With polymer clay, once the cane is built (using opaque material for the star pattern and translucent to fill the voids between the star's points), it is relatively simple to form beads from thick cane slices. After baking, the beads can be buffed and polished until they gleam like glass.

Lampworking is a centuries-old technique for making glass beads with distinctive swirls and nubs of pure color. Traditional glass lampwork beads are made in layers using an open flame and cold rods of colored glass. Seventeenth-century Italian artisans used oil lamps, but today's bead makers employ gas torches. The artist holds a metal rod or wire in one hand and a glass rod in the other. As the glass rod is softened by the flame, the molten color is wound onto the metal rod to make the bead. Raised layers and "eyes" of color are obtained by withdrawing the bead from the flame before the glass becomes fully integrated by the torch.

POLYMER LAMPWORK-STYLE BEADS BY CHERI PYLES

With polymer clay, it is much easier to get the look of lampwork beads. Cheri Pyles uses her fingers rather than a torch to pinch tiny disks of polymer clay and layer them onto a round clay base bead. By not rolling the bead afterward, she preserves the full layered effect. A skewer plays a role similar to that of the metal rod used in glass lampwork; it holds the base bead steady while the colorful embellishments are added.

Glass seed beads have a long tradition in many cultures around the world. They are made in India, Eastern Europe, and now primarily in Japan. Seed beads are usually strung on fine thread and made into strands for jewelry or used as embellishments for embroidery.

TRIO OF BEADS MADE WITH POLYMER SEED BEADS, PIER VOULKOS

Pier Voulkos imitates seed beads by rolling tiny balls of polymer clay in various tints of color. She clusters the balls of clay onto uniquely formed aluminum foil armatures, which make the beads very light in weight and provide many sculptural possibilities. The clay beads adhere to each other and the bead core, and the assembly fuses permanently when baked.

Mosaics made from tiny bits of glass and stone called *tesserae* were constructed by ancient Romans to decorate walls, ceilings, and floors in public houses and the private homes of some wealthy individuals. During the Byzantine era, this technique was adopted and greatly refined. Remarkable detail and dimension were made possible by the subtle gradations of tone among the many millions of tiny tesserae included in a single mosaic.

ASSORTMENT OF CANED MOSAIC BEADS BY STEVEN FORD AND DAVID FORLANO

The caned polymer clay mosaics built by Steven Ford and David Forlano are made from thousands of small tesserae logs in about sixty different colors. The wide range of hues imitates the tonal gradation found in Byzantine mosaics. The approximately square-shaped logs are constructed about the size of French fries and each has a thin layer of clay around it to give the appearance of grout when the image is assembled. Classical geometric mosaic patterns are constructed and caned out to reduce the scale and build the design repeat. Thin slices from the canes are applied as a veneer over cores of solid clay to make beads.

Glass micromosaics were popular in Italy and across Europe in the 17th century. They were made into intricate jewelry, boxes, furniture, and even large copies of famous paintings. Traditional micromosaics are made by pulling threads of hot glass, then cutting the cooled threads into tiny lengths and pressing them one by one onto a wax base to form a two-dimensional image.

MICROMOSAIC BEAD, CYNTHIA TOOPS

Cynthia Toops makes polymer clay micromosaics by pulling threads of polymer clay, baking them, then pressing the pieces into a soft polymer base. Once the design is complete, she bakes it again for permanence. Like her European predecessors, Cynthia works on a painstakingly intricate scale; it often takes her as long as two weeks to complete just one bead.

Turquoise and coral mosaics were created by pre-Columbian Indians of North and Central America. Carolyn Potter imitates this process and appearance with polymer clay and finishes it in a manner similar to contemporary Zuni inlay. She starts by mixing a rich variety of blues and reds to look like turquoise and

PENDANT IN THE STYLE OF ZUNI INLAY, CAROLYN POTTER

coral. Working on a clamshell form, she assembles the design with tiny spaces between the pieces. After the clay is baked, she works a very soft, dark-colored clay into the voids. The piece is rebaked, then sanded smooth and polished.

The heishi technique is an ancient method popular among many cultures for making disk-shaped beads, primarily from shells. The word comes from a Pueblo Indian word for shell bead, and the same technique was applied nearly 30,000 years ago in northern Africa to make disk-shaped beads from ostrich eggshell. Pieces of shell were chipped into circular shapes and drilled in the center with pointed stones. Modern heishi beads are mass produced mechanically, but their slight variations in coloring and thickness reflect the natural materials from which they are made.

HEISHI BRACELETS BY MARIE JOHANNES

The beads in Marie Johannes' bracelets imitate heishi made of turquoise, ivory, coral, and black onyx. They are easily made by rolling the polymer clay around a metal rod, baking, then removing the rod to create a tube of baked clay. The clay tubes are polished with a buffing wheel, then chopped into many short beads of varying thicknesses.

GALLERY

KATHLEEN DUSTIN

"Polymer clay was a natural extension of my ceramic work, which tended to have colorful, highly patterned details. The excitement of using polymer clay comes from its immediacy—you make it, you bake it, you've got it. As I continue exploring new ways of working, I prefer to use methods that serve the concept and visual purpose of my work rather than become bound to any one technique."

ABOVE: *LIFE IS TOUGH FOR PENGUINS*, APPROX. 3" x 4" x 3/4" (7.5 x 10 x 2 CM)

LEFT: *AFTERNOON NAP*, APPROX. 2-1/2" x 3-1/4" x 3/4" (6.5 x 8.5 x 2 CM)

OPPOSITE: *THREE-LEGGED VESSEL*, APPROX. 5-1/2" x 8" x 3-3/4" (14 x 20.5 x 9.5 CM)

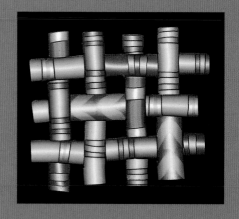

STEVEN FORD AND DAVID FORLANO, CITY ZEN CANE

"Working with this clay is fascinating to me as an artist because it can convincingly imitate so many other materials and techniques, yet still look mysterious and completely new." —D.F.

"I came to polymer clay after working in glass and paint. This unique material seems to join those two interests in a totally new way that is seductive, direct, and endless. Just when I think that I've exhausted the possibilities of caning, something new happens, and it all opens up again." —S.F.

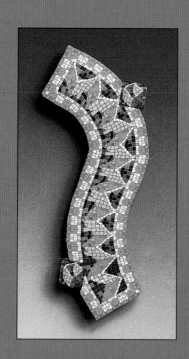

ABOVE: NECKLACE, APPROX. 25" (63.5 CM) LONG
OPPOSITE TOP LEFT: PIN, APPROX. 2" x 2-1/2" (5 x 6.5 CM)
OPPOSITE TOP RIGHT: PIN, APPROX. 1-1/2" x 3-3/4" (4 x 9.5 CM)
OPPOSITE BOTTOM: FRAMES, APPROX. 8" x 10" (20.5 x 25.5 CM) AND 7-1/2" x 6" (18 x 15 CM)

WILCKE SMITH

"My works suggesting enigmatic beings in vanished worlds were long done with fiber. Then I saw the awesome work being done in polymer clay and decided that clay and fiber are congenial materials. Now I choose polymer clay, with its elegant matte surface and wondrous ability to meld colors, when it best expresses my ideas."

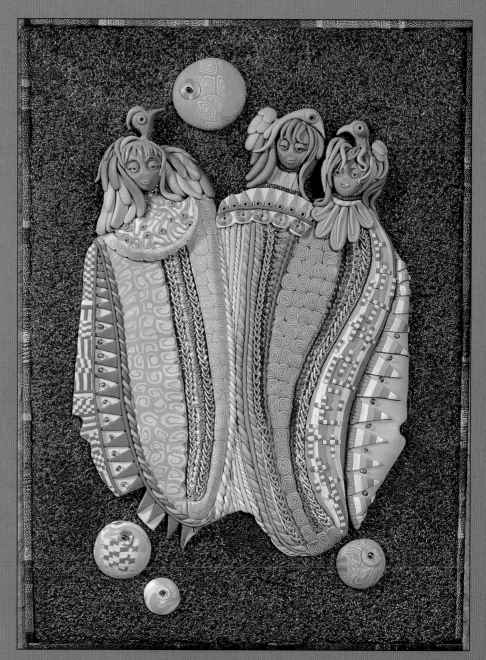

MOONDANCE, 9" x 12" (23 x 30.5 CM); PHOTO BY BOB SMITH

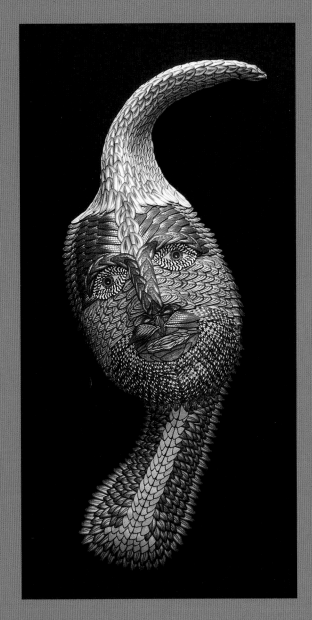

RUTH ANNE AND
MICHAEL GROVE

"As a painter, I love working with
color. Polymer clay gives me the
opportunity to explore texture and
three-dimensional form while using
color."—R.G.

"I enjoy the tactile qualities of clay,
its texture and feel. It also provides a
context for me to investigate a rich
range of colors and patterns."—M.G.

ABOVE: *WHO WILL REMEMBER MY TROUBLES
WHEN I'M GONE*, MICHAEL GROVE, APPROX.
10" x 26" x 6-1/2" DEEP (25.5 x 66 x 16.5 CM);
PHOTO BY MICHAEL GROVE

RIGHT: *TOP OF THE CHAIN*, RUTH ANNE GROVE,
APPROX. 17" x 20" x 6" DEEP (43 x 51 x 15 CM);
PHOTO BY MICHAEL GROVE

SARAH LEE

"Vibrant blocks of color, tactile appeal, infinite potential...I'm hooked! The more I experience working with polymer clay, the more excited I become with its boundless versatility."

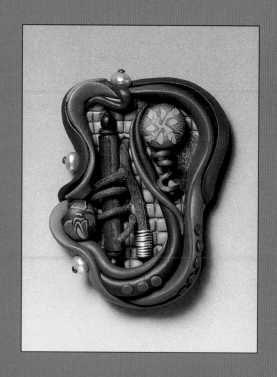

TOP: PIN, APPROX.
1-1/2" x 2-1/2"
(4 x 6.5 CM)

LEFT: BOTTLES,
APPROX. 1/2" DIA. X
4" (1.5 x 10 CM)

Necklace, approx. 24" (61 cm) long

TAMELA WELLS LAITY

"I happened on to polymer clay as I was looking for a way to introduce color into my sterling silver designs. As I experimented with the material, it seemed one idea rapidly led to another. What began as a hobby and 'fun time' secondary to my silver work soon became the primary outlet for my creative energy."

"Polymer clay provides instant gratification for a doll maker. There is no time wasted on mold processes, and it's wonderful to have no loss of shape due to shrinking from kiln firing. All of a sudden we can do anything from elves to old ladies…and we do."

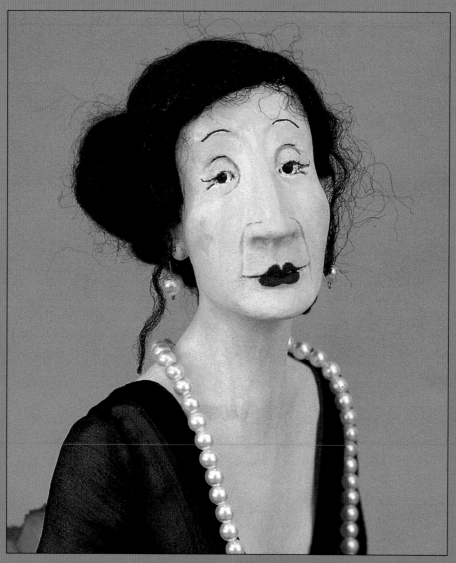

DAPHNE, APPROX. 12" (30.5 CM) HIGH, SEATED; PHOTO BY W. DON SMITH

MAGGIE RUDY

"I started modeling with polymer clay as a means to explore three-dimensional work at home. What excites me most about the material is its versatility and speed. I can work out an idea and have it fired in a few hours. If everyone were issued a package of polymer clay at birth, we would all grow up to be well adjusted and happy."

ABOVE: DETAIL, *JERRY RUDY*, PHOTO BY BILL BACHHUBER

RIGHT: *JERRY RUDY*, APPROX. 16" (40.5 CM) TALL; PHOTO BY BILL BACHHUBER

LIZ MITCHELL

"In my work I try to create the same sense of wonderment about the world that I felt when I was growing up. I try to express humor and lightheartedness, and my work is intended to generate a smile and a sense of enjoyment."

ORNAMENT, APPROX. 6" x 2-1/2" x 1-1/2" (15 x 6.5 x 4 CM)

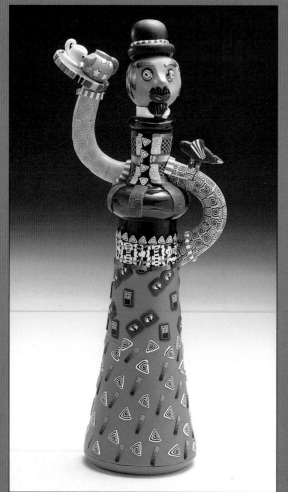

LAURA BALOMBINI

"When I was working in ceramics in the early 1970s, I was taken by the bright colors and speed of low-fire clay and glazes but was unhappy with the limited palette. When I found polymer clay and started mixing colors, fireworks went off in my imagination. I love a challenge."

A LITTLE MAGIC WITH YOUR TEA?, APPROX. 2-1/2" DIA. x 9" (6.5 x 23 CM)

BOTTLES, APPROX. 3-3/4" x 5-1/2" x 1-3/4" (9.5 x 14 x 4.5 CM)

KARYN KOZAK

"Working with polymer clay gives me a wide range of saturated color and the ability to hold detail. The challenge, as in all aspects of life, is in deciding which details to pay attention to and which to discard."

ALAN SLESINGER

"Being an impatient person, what I like most about polymer clay is the quick results I get. By repeatedly manipulating colors, then putting them under light, I can get a depth and diversity of color that are really marvelous. I enjoy pushing the material to an extreme and moving in a direction that nobody has gone before."

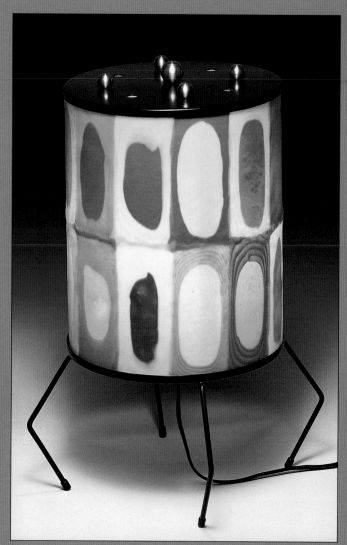

Lamp, approx. 8" dia. x 16" (20.5 x 40.5 cm)

Clock, approx. 8" x 12-1/2" (20.5 x 32 cm)

MICHELE FANNER

"I started using polymer clay in an effort to produce original buttons that wouldn't crack or chip for use in my own knitwear designs. My search for the 'perfect button' is still a driving force behind my work."

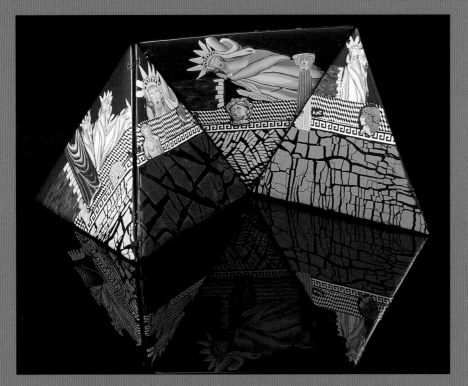

KATHLEEN AMT

"I love this material! I continue to ask it to do new things, and it reveals more than I could have imagined. I push. It shoves back."

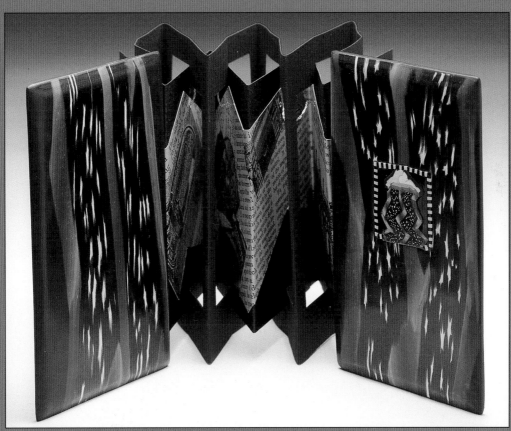

TOP: *Has Liberty Lost Her Fire?*, EACH TRIANGLE 6" (15 CM) ON ALL SIDES
BOTTOM: *Highly Charged*, APPROX. 3-1/4" x 5-1/4" (8.5 x 13.5 CM), CLOSED

THE DAY BEFORE MY BIRTHDAY, APPROX. 5-1/2" x 5-1/4" (14 x 13.5 CM)

LIZ MACK

"As a photographer I built my images in the darkroom, color by color, taking up to 3-1/2 hours in total darkness to execute a single print. Working with polymer clay allows me to be just as experimental with color mixing and texturing, without the handicap of darkness and with greater spontaneity."

CLAIRE LATIES DAVIS

"Most recently I have been working with the combined painterly and sculptural possibilities of polymer clay. I love being able to sculpt evocative faces and gestures, blend colors, and incorporate textures all within the same medium."

TOP:
ASIAN FAMILY, APPROX. 4-3/4" x 6-1/4" (12 x 16 CM)

RIGHT:
THREE LITTLE BOYS, APPROX. 7-1/4" x 5-1/4" (18.5 x 13.5 CM)

PIER VOULKOS

"Polymer clay's relatively short history is one of its attractions; I get to invent my own rules as I go along. Each time I start a project, I play with a whole new set of unknowns. Even after years of experience with the material, I'm constantly presented with new directions to explore."

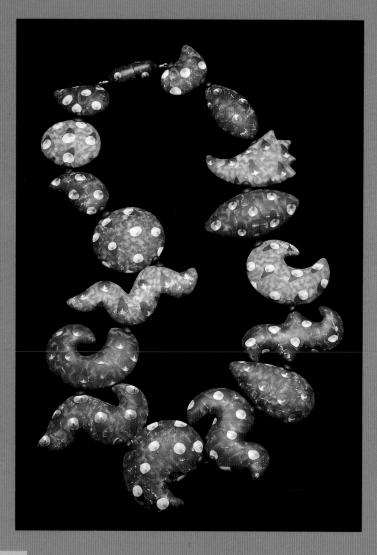

ABOVE: MIRROR, APPROX. 8" x 10-1/2" (20.5 x 26.5 CM)

LEFT: SHAPED BEADS NECKLACE, APPROX. 24" (61 CM) LONG

OPPOSITE TOP: SHORT SHELL BEADS NECKLACE, APPROX. 20" (51 CM) LONG

OPPOSITE BOTTOM: FANCY FALL LEAF NECKLACE, APPROX. 19" (48.5 CM) LONG

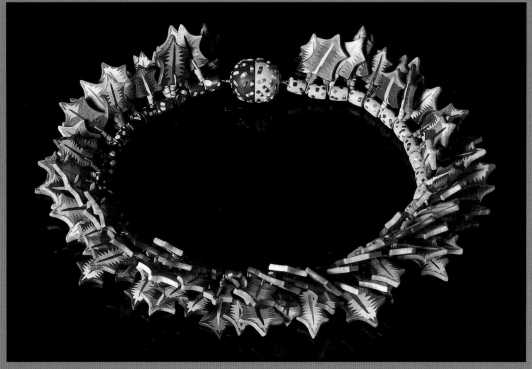

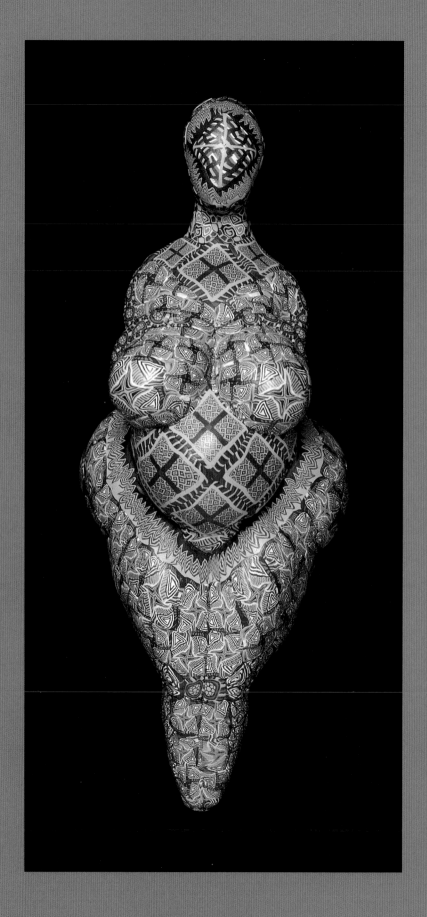

CAROLYN POTTER

"My work in polymer clay is a natural extension of my experience with ceramic clays. In fact, my interest in millefiori as a ceramic technique brought me to polymer clay canes. Polymer clay has taught me more about color than any other media, and canework has made it possible for me to cover my sculptures in color and pattern."

FERTILITY GODDESS, APPROX. 8-1/2" (21.5 CM) HIGH

CYNTHIA TOOPS

"The infinite color palette and textures that can be achieved with polymer clay are what keep me drawn to it. Its portability is another real plus; when cabin fever sets in (quite often), I just pack up my supplies and head off to 'bead' at my favorite coffee shop."

TOP: BROOCH, APPROX. 2-1/4" x 3" (5.5 x 7.5 CM)
LEFT: BEAD, APPROX. 1-1/2" x 1-3/4" (4 x 4.5 CM)

TORY HUGHES

"In polymer clay, everything is possible, and the overt purpose of using imitative techniques is to be able to create any object or effect you desire. Equally important is the delight in making things that are not themselves recognizable but that have recognizable characteristics. Experiment and trust your instincts; there are no mistakes."

OPPOSITE: BOWL, APPROX. 4-1/4" DIA. x 2"
(11 x 5 CM)

RIGHT: PENDANT, APPROX. 1-1/4" x 4-1/4"
(3 x 11 CM)

BELOW: FOOTED BOWL, APPROX. 5" DIA. x 2"
(12.5 x 5 CM)

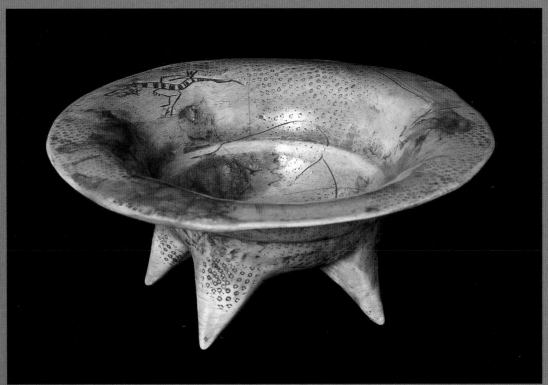

lthough polymer clay hasn't quite become a household term yet, the recent explosion of creative work has made it much more familiar. Scores of artists and home crafters have been drawn to this relatively new medium by its color and versatility.

The name polymer clay reveals an apparent contradiction in its nature: it's a manmade substance—a plastic—yet it has many characteristics common to natural materials. Like ceramic clay, it is very pliable in its initial state and can be fired to a permanent hardness with the application of heat. The fact that its color is throughout the material, not added later to the surface, makes it similar to glass.

Unlike either of these two media, polymer clay requires no high-temperature furnace or kiln, nor any special tools for handling. And it doesn't have the fragility of glass or ceramics. It can be molded, sculpted, formed into intricate patterns, and manipulated in dozens of ways by hand, then baked in a standard kitchen oven to achieve permanence. The low temperature required for firing—from 212 to 275 degrees Fahrenheit (100 to 135 degrees Centigrade)—means that anyone can work easily and safely with this material.

Polymer clay is readily available from craft stores and through mail-order suppliers. It comes in small blocks, generally about two ounces (57 grams) each, and in bulk quantities. Several brands are sold, and due to the rapidly increasing popularity of this material, polymer clay with new qualities and additional brands of clay may be expected to follow.

BRAND CHARACTERISTICS

Essentially all polymer clays are alike; they all contain varying amounts of polyvinyl chloride (PVC), plasticizer, and color pigments. The similarity among brands is a real advantage because you can combine different brands to achieve the colors, textures, and other qualities you like. At the same time, the variations in formula give each type of polymer clay unique characteristics.

Sculpey III, manufactured by Polyform Products Company, is relatively soft in texture and can be used immediately without much kneading or conditioning. When handled extensively, it can become too soft to hold crisp detail and must be cooled to restore some stiffness. Unfired Sculpey can be stored for long periods without becoming hard. When baked it has a beautiful matte finish, although it seems to have less strength than other brands.

Pro-Mat is also produced by Polyform Products Company. It has a rubbery texture and is noted for its higher strength. Pro-Mat comes in larger, four-ounce (113-gram) blocks and features superb gold and silver metallic clays. When baked in combination with Sculpey III, it makes wonderful molds that release pressed polymer easily.

Cernit is a product of T & F GmbH. After baking, it has the best rigid strength of any clay but doesn't flex as well as other brands. It's good for basic patterns, and it's probably the best choice for very thin clay structures. When fully conditioned, Cernit can be sticky or tacky to handle. Baking significantly alters the appearance of this clay, giving it a porcelainlike finish. Its naturalistic flesh tones make it a popular choice among doll makers.

Manufactured by Eberhard Faber, Fimo has good strength and flexibility when baked. Relative to other brands, its initial consistency is quite stiff, and it requires thorough conditioning before it becomes workable. This stiffer, somewhat rubbery quality makes Fimo especially good for very fine detail and canework. Among its many colors, Fimo includes

AN ASSORTMENT OF POLYMER CLAY BRANDS

art translucent, which is the most translucent clay of any brand available.

Friendly Clay, made by American Art Clay Company, is softer than Fimo and firmer than Sculpey III. Unlike Sculpey III, which continues to soften as it's being worked (after it has been conditioned), Friendly Clay softens to a point, then maintains its firmness. Its ability to hold detail makes it a good choice for canework, and it is relatively strong when baked.

Modello is produced in Germany for Dryad in England, and in the United States, it is sold under the product name of Formello. This clay is similar to Fimo but is much softer. It holds fine detail in a cane, requires little kneading, and has some wonderful colors, but it is often difficult to find.

CONDITIONING

To achieve good results with polymer clay, you must condition the material until it has a uniform consistency. Every brand, even the softest, is somewhat stiff right out of the package, and within a single brand, some colors tend to be stiffer than others. There are several ways to condition clay, and you can mix brands to create the consistency you prefer. Once clay has been properly conditioned, you can store it for as long as a week, depending on the temperature, before it loses its working consistency and must be conditioned again.

Starting with a small amount at one time, warm the clay in your hand or with something else—hot water bottles, electric heating pads, warming trays, or sunny windowsills. When you warm the clay mechanically, be careful to insulate it from the heat source with a towel. If the clay becomes too warm, it will begin to harden. (Sitting too long in a sunny window can harden it too.) Wrap the clay in some waxed paper before putting it in the towel to keep it from picking up lint and to prevent the plasticizer from leaching into the absorbent towel.

To condition the clay, roll a small amount into a ball, then into a log. Stretch and roll out the clay until it is very long; then fold it back on itself. Twist, roll, and repeat until the clay is of an even consistency and color. Now roll the clay into a ball and store it until needed. This method is ideal for small batches of clay—and for exercising your hand muscles.

When conditioning more than one color at one sitting, don't worry about small flecks of one color "contaminating" another. By the time the clay has been thoroughly kneaded, these will have disappeared.

For larger batches of clay, or to avoid hand fatigue, try using two common kitchen tools not designed for polymer clay. Grind the clay with a food processor and knead it with a pasta machine to mix colors and condition the clay simultaneously. A coffee grinder may be substituted for the more expensive food processor, but it can handle only small amounts at one time. Once used for this purpose, it is very important to dedicate this equipment solely to polymer clay. Do not use the processor bowl or blade or the pasta machine for food after it has been used to mix clay. If you don't want the expense and bulk of having two complete food processors, buy an inexpensive second bowl and blade to use only for clay.

To condition clay by machine, begin by cutting it into pieces about the size of sugar cubes or smaller (photo 1). Fill the food processor bowl only half full at most so that you don't risk damaging the machine. Remember, these machines weren't designed for this! You can mix any number of colors together at this stage—just throw them into the bowl.

In colder climates and with certain brands, especially Fimo, the clay might feel very stiff. Add a few drops of mineral oil or one of the commercial thinners such as Fimo Mix Quick or Sculpey Diluent as an ingredient in the mix to help soften the clay. When fluorescent or translucent colors are included, it isn't necessary to add any softeners because these

2

colors tend to have a waxy consistency of their own.

Grind the clay in the processor for a full minute or two (photo 2). This not only chops the clay into small grains and disperses the colors evenly throughout the mixture, but the friction of the clay spinning in the bowl also warms and softens the clay considerably. Stop the machine if the clay starts to clump. Often you can hear when the clay is ready by the change in motor sound.

Empty the clay onto a work surface and form a ball. It will have been conditioned from the grinding, so roll it out immediately while the clay is soft and warm. Use a roller of some type—a dedicated rolling pin, acrylic cylinder, or a brayer—to flatten the clay to a thickness approximately equal to that of the widest setting on the pasta machine (photos 3 and 4). This is an important step and shouldn't be overlooked. If you don't flatten the clay enough by hand, the pasta machine will only shred it for you.

After rolling it through the machine at the widest setting, reduce the setting by one and send it through again. Do this once more. You will notice that as the clay gets thinner and the piece longer, the texture of the clay becomes more plastic (photo 5). Fold the clay sheet in half onto itself and send it, fold first, through without changing the setting. The settings on pasta machines vary by manufacturer, but kneading on the thinner settings (usually the higher numbers) is the fastest way to condition polymer clay. Repeat the fold-and-roll process until the clay has an even color and texture. Changing directions each time you send the material through

3

4

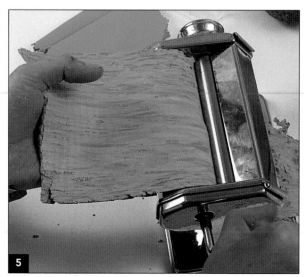

5

the machine will hasten the process. Ball it up or leave it in sheet form for future use.

If the clay is too soft for what you want to do, you might combine it with a stiffer clay. Alternatively, you can blot out the excess plasticizer by flattening the clay into a sheet and laying it on an absorbent surface overnight. With less plasticizer, the clay will be stiffer. Clean blank newsprint works very well, but don't use printed newspaper because the ink will transfer to your clay. Chilling polymer clay will also stiffen it, but only temporarily.

MIXING AND USING COLORS

Mixing your own color palette is one of the most pleasurable aspects of this medium. Many of the colors available are highly saturated (intense), so you have plenty of options for making a full range of hues. All brands offer a variety of tints, but you can make any color you choose, from the palest pastel to the deepest jewel tone, by combining various amounts of the primary colors—red, yellow, and blue—and by adding black and white.

Follow the basics of color theory and don't combine equal amounts of complementary colors such as red and green, yellow and purple, or orange and blue. (If you're unsure about which colors are complementary, look at a color wheel; these are the hues that are opposite each other on the wheel.) As they do with paint, these combinations make gray. Occasionally you may find it advantageous to add just a bit of a complementary color to lessen the intensity of your chosen shade.

When mixing your own colors, always start with the lighter clay and add small amounts of the darker one. It's easy to darken a color, but much more difficult to lighten it. Red and black are particularly intense colors, so be extra cautious about adding these to your mixture.

Adding white to a color lightens it by making it pastel. If you want to retain the true color but lessen its impact, you can "thin" it by using translucent clay. Again, start with the translucent and add small amounts of color until you have the effect you want.

Fluorescent hues are semitransparent and, on their own, look garish. When included as ingredients in a custom color mixture, they can pump up the intensity of the hue and brighten your palette without whitening it. As a rule of thumb, no more than about one-third of your total mix should be fluorescent clay.

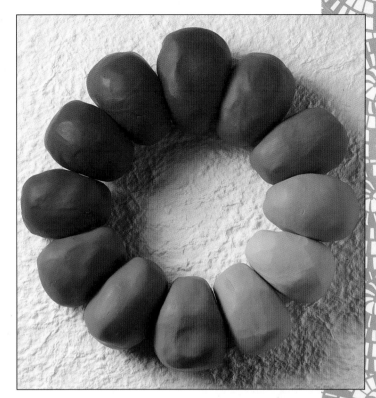

A POLYMER CLAY COLOR WHEEL MADE BY DAVID FORLANO

Some colors change slightly when they're baked; navy blue looks black, and red becomes brick red. The colors affected by baking are basically the same ones—reds, blues, and some yellows—regardless of brand. It might be wise to bake small samples of the colors that you plan to use. Often colors that are mixed using several ingredients will change because one of the ingredients is affected by baking. If a desired color does darken, add a little white or lighter shade of the same color to hold the saturation that you desire.

To replicate an especially pleasing color later, it helps if you've kept track of your mixing ratios. In fact, some people like to create color charts that include baked slices of their favorite colors together with the formulas for mixing them.

Incomplete mixtures of two or more colors can result in some interesting effects that resemble marbled designs or the colored linoleum tiles from the 1950s. If this is your goal, it's best to condition all of the colors separately before mixing to ensure an even consistency. Partial mixing by machine (food processor plus pasta machine) results in mottled effects; for more definitive striping of colors, mix them by hand. Start with logs of each color and spiral them together into a candy cane. Roll this into a ball and continue manipulating it from ball to log to ball until you have a pattern you enjoy.

When choosing colors for your project, first decide what impression you want to make. Do you want one color to predominate, or should it share equally with the others? Color relationships affect both the mood and spatial perception of a design. A contrast of cool colors, which recede, against warm ones, which advance, creates a vibrancy that is exciting; subtle variations in value (lightness or darkness of a color) produce three-dimensional effects. One last thought on the subject of color: if your designs tend to be small and intricate, try to err on the side of boldness rather than subtlety. From a distance, the eye tends to blend the colors it perceives and may miss overly delicate distinctions.

If you're having trouble assembling a personal color palette, take a look in your closet. Mix a range of the colors you like to wear and add an occasional bold accent.

TOOLS

There are very few tools that are absolute necessities for working with polymer clay, and all are easy to obtain. The most important tools are ones you have with you at all times—your hands. With your hands you can roll perfectly round beads, shape flat sheets into intricate forms, and construct detailed designs. All it takes is a little practice.

Because polymer clay is such a tactile material, most people prefer to work with bare hands. If you don't like having clay residue on your skin or if leaving your fingerprints on the clay becomes a problem, you can purchase thin latex examination gloves at many drug stores.

Your work surface can be any nonporous material that is smooth and flat. Plastic laminates and bristol board are best because they have very fine textures that easily release the clay as you work with it. Slick surfaces such as glass and acrylics tend to adhere to polymer clay and make it more difficult to handle. Any surface is more convenient if cut into a sheet that can be put aside when not in use.

You have many choices for cutting polymer clay. One essential tool is a sharp, flat blade to make precise cuts. A craft knife works well for some applications, but it's likely that you will need a longer cutting surface for many of your projects.

For these, a wallpaper scraping blade is better and a tissue-slicing blade is best of all. The latter can be purchased from some craft suppliers and from medical supply houses.

Flattening clay into sheets requires a roller of some sort—an old rolling pin that has been dedicated to art, an acrylic tube, a long cylindrical glass, or a brayer. Polymer clay tends to stick to wood more readily than it does to acrylic plastic, but you can alleviate this by coating your rolling pin with polyurethane. If your projects call for numerous sheets of clay in consistent thicknesses, consider buying a pasta machine. Not only is it useful for conditioning and blending clay, but it can also produce miles of clay sheets in a variety of thicknesses, some much thinner than you can easily achieve by hand.

Piercing tools are useful if you plan to make beads. Darning needles, wooden skewers, and fine knitting needles can all apply holes to unbaked clay. With some bead shapes, there is an advantage to baking first, then drilling holes with an electric drill and small bits to prevent distortion of the design.

Other tools to consider include found objects, fountain pen nibs, sculpting tools, dental tools, container caps, and whatever else comes to hand. Unbaked polymer clay is so malleable that you can texture it, incise it, or model it with just about anything.

For baking you'll need a regular home oven (*not* a microwave) and something on which to set your pieces. Beads and other round objects should be suspended to avoid flattening them on one side. Other projects can be baked on any nonglossy flat surface. A baking sheet or pan made of metal or glass tends to produce a shiny surface where it touches the clay. To avoid this, place your projects on a sheet of 100 percent rag paper (which is acid free and won't discolor your work during baking), oven parchment, or thin cardboard. Since the clay tends to sag as it gets warmer, some pieces may need support structures to hold them in shape during baking.

Temperature control during baking is very important. Underbaking results in incomplete polymerization, hence lower strength, and overbaking can burn the clay. Both full-sized and toaster ovens tend to fluctuate in temperature, and some are quite inaccurate. To be sure of the temperature during the baking cycle, periodically check your oven with an oven thermometer and make any necessary adjustments.

Tools for working with polymer clay, left to right in rows: pasta machine, oven thermometer, sanding and buffing wheel, sanding screens, steel wool, food processor bowl and blade, clay extruder, wood and plexiglass rollers, brayer, jewelers' saw, latex examination gloves, metal snips, wire cutter, clay manipulating tools, chain-nose pliers, round-nose pliers, wallpaper scraping blade, tissue blade, craft knife, file

SURFACE TREATMENTS: METALLIC PAINT AND POWDERS, COLORED PENCILS, GOLD AND COPPER METAL LEAF, METALLIC RUBBING COMPOUND

Your options don't end once a piece is baked. Most important, you can add unbaked clay to modify or extend the construction of your work and bake it again. And again and again, if you wish. Once it has cooled, you can drill, sand, and polish the clay. Surface treatments such as acrylic paints and water-color pencils can also be applied. If desired, other materials and findings, such as pin backs and bar-rette clips, can be glued in place.

BAKING

Your last step before baking should be to look over your project carefully and fix any imperfections that you find. Telltale signs of a piece that was rushed into the oven include fingerprints, pieces of dirt, and bub-bles in the clay. The latter are especially troublesome because they can expand during baking. Prick them with a fine needle and smooth out the trapped air.

There are many opinions about baking times and temperatures among artists who work with polymer clay. Follow the manufacturer's guidelines on the package, but if you're unhappy with the strength, try a *slightly* higher temperature and/or longer bak-ing time to cure the clay more fully.

STORAGE

Because it isn't water soluble, polymer clay won't dry out over the short run, even if it is left uncov-ered. When wrapped, its shelf life is at least two years and can be considerably longer. Sculpey III seems to last the longest, and some artists doing canework favor it because they can keep a larger

selection of canes made over a period of time. A conditioned piece of clay does become stiffer after it has sat for several days, so you should avoid com-bining older designs with fresh ones if you don't want uneven consistency.

Polymer clay is heat activated and can begin to harden if left in a sunny spot. It's best to store your clay in a cool, dry place and wrap it so that the colors don't stick together.

To prevent an accumulation of dust on your materi-al and make it last longer, store it in airtight contain-ers. Some plastics may be susceptible to the plasti-cizer, which tends to leach out, and stick to the clay. A sheet of waxed paper provides good insurance against this.

GENERAL SAFETY

All of the manufacturers insist that when used as directed there are no health risks associated with their products. Polymer clay is certified nontoxic, but you should take some commonsense precautions to minimize your exposure to any chemical ingredi-ents in this and other artists' materials.

Any tools used for your craft—pasta machines, food processors, coffee grinders, rollers, or knives—should never be returned to kitchen duty afterward. Use rubber gloves or make sure to clean your hands thoroughly when you have finished working with the clay. If wearing rubber gloves is uncomfortable for some work, use them for the big jobs such as mixing clay, where the sensitivity of touch is less important. When sanding and polishing baked clay to get a smoother surface, wear a good quality dust mask or wet-sand them.

When the clay is baked at the proper temperature, it creates an odor. This is to be expected. Whether you enjoy the smell or merely tolerate it, be sure to use good ventilation while baking. Hazardous fumes can be produced if the temperature exceeds the rec-ommended limits and the material burns. If you experience an acrid, burning smell that is noticeably different from the norm, turn off the oven, throw open the windows, and go somewhere else until the odor has dissipated.

Some of the metallic finishes used with polymer clay can be hazardous if handled improperly. Always fol-low the manufacturer's instructions carefully and use protective equipment when indicated. Even small amounts of these materials can irritate sensitive skin.

rtists who work with polymer clay have developed many innovative techniques for taking advantage of the qualities unique to this material. Some methods exploit the more obvious properties of color and malleability; others rely on its chemical nature and its ability to be baked over and over again. Not to be forgotten are the techniques that have been discovered purely by accident.

As you gain experience with the material, you will develop a personal style and become comfortable with certain techniques. Use the ideas presented here, along with your own experience with other processes and materials, as a springboard for making new discoveries about this ever-changing medium.

BASIC SHAPES

Don't assume that you need complicated techniques to produce beautiful results. Some of the most effective designs are those that use simple techniques and basic shapes.

In fact, the ability to make round balls, flat sheets, and cylindrical logs in a variety of sizes is an absolute necessity if you're to be successful with other techniques. Take the time to practice rolling perfect spheres in the palms of your hands. Then convert these to logs by rolling them on your work surface. Your logs will be more consistent in diameter if you use the flatter part of your hand rather than your fingers to roll the clay.

To flatten clay into sheets without a pasta machine, roll one or two strokes in each direction with a roller or brayer. Then lift the clay and turn it over. Frequent turning as you flatten the clay will keep it from sticking to your work surface. You'll get an even thickness by placing a strip of wood on either side of the clay. The strips will act as guides for your roller and prevent you from getting thin areas.

Make a sphere into a bead by piercing it with a sharp needle. (If a larger hole is desired, enlarge the existing hole with a skewer, knitting needle, or other tool.) Roll the needle between your fingers as you insert it to minimize distortion; then reinsert the needle from the other end of the hole to eliminate

any small bump of clay that may have formed there (figure 1). Use the same twisting motion to pierce a cylindrical bead or wafer bead cut from a log of clay. If your clay is soft and easily distorted by the needle, let it rest and cool for several hours.

Figure 1

Z Kripke's round and wafer beads are decorated with thin slices from slabs that are made with multiple layers of graded tones. Careful positioning of the

BEADED NECKLACE, BRACELET, AND EARRING BY Z KRIPKE

light and dark portions of the slices to imply the over-and-under effect of weaving gives sparkle and movement to these simple bead shapes.

Combinations of simple shapes can produce complex images such as the turquoise and coral mosaics by Carolyn Potter. Tiny rectangular pieces of clay are assembled into the desired pattern on a premade form, in this case a clamshell. Reflecting traditional mosaic work, small gaps are left between the individual pieces of clay. After baking, the gaps can be filled in with a very soft clay "grout" and rebaked, sanded, and polished, or the piece can be left as is for a more textural effect.

VESSEL WITH INCISED PATTERNS AND INLAY, TORY HUGHES, APPROX. 2-1/4" DIA. x 3-1/2" (5.5 x 9 CM)

CLAMSHELL MOSAIC PENDANT, CAROLYN POTTER, APPROX. 3" x 2-1/2" (7.5 x 6.5 CM)

INCISED DESIGNS

You can get a range of linear effects by incising baked and unbaked clay. Both methods have advantages, depending upon what effects you want to achieve. Lines cut into an unbaked slab of clay have smooth edges and a cleaner look; lines cut into baked cay using a craft knife or V-shaped gouging tool have ragged edges and appear cruder. (Cutting baked polymer clay is similar to cutting the linoleum used for making prints.) To affect the quality of your line, vary the tools. Try a nail or saw blade in baked clay, or drag a comb into unbaked clay. Nearly anything can be used to create a textural design in polymer clay. Try pressing soft clay with

pieces of coarsely woven cloth, seashells, coins, sandpaper, screws, string, foil, even your own baked clay creations.

The designs in the vessel by Tory Hughes were carved into the clay after it was baked. Most of the patterns were deeply and boldly incised, but some were lightly scratched into the clay to add depth to the overall design. Small pieces of prebaked turquoise and coral clay were inlaid before the main vessel was baked.

Other possibilities include impressing raw clay with metal type or repeatedly poking pointed objects into it to achieve a stippled effect. Metal type is cast backward so that it will print correctly when pressed onto a surface. Linda Soberman's portrait and pin combine incising techniques with transfer images and molding.

Incised patterns generally look more dramatic with the addition of a *patina*. The term patina refers to a

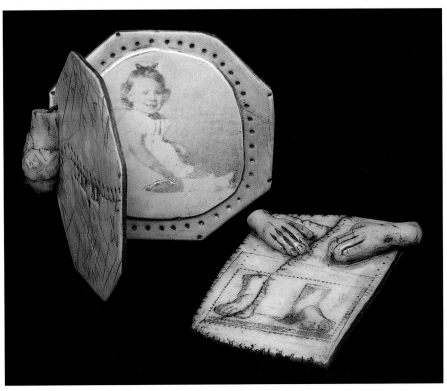

PORTRAIT, APPROX. 3" X 3" (7.5 X 7.5 CM), AND PIN, APPROX. 2" X 3" (5 X 7.5 CM), BY LINDA SOBERMAN

Nan Roche's pendants employ animal imagery from copyright-free design books. You can also transfer your own drawings and photographs. Make a photocopy of the image you want to transfer and place it face down onto unbaked clay, making sure that there is full contact (and no air bubbles) between the image and the clay. White or near-white clay will show the image best, but other colors can be used too. Let it rest for about a half-hour; then carefully peel away the paper from one corner. This technique works best with fresh photocopies or copies on plastic film (transparencies).

traditional method for enhancing the surface color of metal through a chemical reaction, either natural (such as the verdigris created when copper oxidizes) or manmade (using chemically reactive paints). Patinas can give new materials the worn look of antiques. With polymer clay you can use water-based paints or stains to achieve similar, striking results. After the piece has been baked, simply paint on a thin layer of a dark color and work it into all the cracks, fissures, and surface textures. Then take off as much of the paint as you can with steel wool or a buffing wheel, leaving only traces of the patina in the crevices.

IMAGE TRANSFERS

The presence of plasticizer in polymer clay makes it possible to transfer ink and the images from photocopies. The first person to discover this probably cursed at the unforeseen pollution of his fresh clay, but the creative use of transfer images—both color and black and white—offers a wide range of possibilities. Just keep in mind that the transfer copy is a mirror image of the original; any printed words will be backwards.

PENDANTS BY NAN ROCHE, EACH APPROX. 2-1/2" X 2" (6.5 X 5 CM)

SURFACE TREATMENTS

Metal leaf and metallic paints and powders stick easily to unbaked polymer clay. Metal leaf is available in a range of colors—gold, silver, copper, bronze, and aluminum. All metal leaf is extremely fragile and tears easily when handled, and most types (those other than true gold) can also tarnish if you touch them with your bare hands. To avoid handling the leaf directly, use a lightly moistened artists' brush to lift the leaf gently into place.

One approach for using metal leaf is to lay it onto a sheet of clay and roll it by hand or run it through the pasta machine. Rolling stretches the clay and breaks up the surface of the metal leaf, producing a natural effect. Thessaly Barnett's pendant is woven from strips of clay that sparkle with bits of gold leaf. (Unbaked polymer clay—especially Fimo and Pro-Mat, which have a rubbery quality—is quite flexible and can easily be woven, folded, or ruffled.)

Another method is to use solid sheets of metal leaf as layers in striped loaves. Incised marks in the delicately rendered floral letter openers by Lindly

LETTER OPENERS BY LINDLY HAUNANI, EACH APPROX. 1-1/4" x 3-1/4" (3 x 8.5 CM)

WOVEN POLYMER CLAY PENDANT, THESSALY BARNETT, APPROX. 3" x 3" (7.5 x 7.5 CM)

SPIRIT GODDESS, LYNNE SWARD, APPROX. 1-1/4" x 4" (3 x 10 CM)

Face pin, Marguerite Kuhl, approx. 2" x 2-1/4" (5 x 5.5 cm)

Haunani reveal a subtle hint of the silver leaf trapped between thin layers of translucent clay.

The figurative pins by Marg Kuhl and Lynne Sward have gold and other colored metallic powders rubbed into the textured surface of the clay. Metallic powders can be applied to smooth clay, too, as demonstrated by Wilcke Smith's "guardians." For additional enhancement, you can incorporate metallic fibers and fabric to complement the powders.

Masks by Anna Riddile, from 1" (2.5 cm) to 2" (5 cm) tall

Guardians, Wilcke Smith, approx. 5" (12.5 cm) tall; photo by Bob Smith

Colored pencil applied after baking provides unique surface texture and coloring to Anna Riddile's bead-sized mask images. Try scrubbing light colors onto heavily textured dark clay bases for an effect similar to oil pastels. Darker colors show better on white or light-colored clays. Don't use any markers, paints, or oil pastels that might have a solvent base. They might react with the plasticizer in polymer clay, even after baking, and make a sticky mess.

A NECKLACE "SAMPLER" OF BEADS USING IMITATIVE AND INCISING TECHNIQUES BY MARIE JOHANNES, APPROX. 42" (106.5 CM) LONG

SIMULATING NATURAL MATERIALS

One of polymer clay's more remarkable properties is its ability to make convincing imitations of natural materials such as jade, ivory, turquoise, coral, and marble. Gradations of tone, contrasting veins, and random imperfections are easily achieved for naturalistic effects. This technique was first developed and perfected by Tory Hughes (see page 32), and it can be applied equally successfully to imitations of actual materials and to creations that look real but are strictly imaginary.

By alternating thin layers of ivory-colored opaque clay with thin layers of translucent clay, you can create the subtle grain of natural ivory. Mixing a tiny amount of opaque clay into a large portion of translucent clay produces a thin color "wash" that effectively imitates the translucency of jade and some of the veins found in marble. Remember to mix various shades of the same color, since most natural materials have a combination of hues.

Most of the beads in Marie Johannes' necklace imitate natural materials, and you can identify jade, ivory, wood, turquoise, amber, coral, stone, terra cotta, and ceramic stoneware. Many exploit a variety of finishing techniques that you can employ after the clay has been baked. Some have marks and lines that were carved after baking, and others include patterns that were pressed into unbaked clay. Try using a wood carving tool or one of the many fittings for a miniature electric engraving and grinding tool.

You can build textural variety in a single design by impressing part of the clay, baking the piece, then carving the hardened clay. Finally, polish the surface with a buffing wheel. The buffing wheel can't reach the deep impressions, and these will keep their duller surface.

PRESS MOLDS

Polymer clay's suppleness and fine grain make it ideal for molding detailed forms. Molds are great tools for producing multiples of the same design or for creating a complex shape without having to sculpt it by hand. The ability of polymer clay to show fine detail is demonstrated in Maggie Rudy's apple box, which exhibits every slight bruise evident in the original fruit from which it was molded. Donna Kato's sumo face pin shows the effectiveness of combining molded forms with other techniques.

A mixture of Pro-Mat and Sculpey III produces good molds that release easily, and a product called Super Elasticlay (part of the Sculpey family) makes molds that remain rubbery even after baking. The stretchy quality of Super Elasticlay makes the mold easy to release from the soft, unbaked clay.

When making a mold, you will have better results if you apply talcum powder to the surface of the object you wish to cast. Press the object gently and evenly into the clay to make a mold with good detail. After baking the mold, dust the inside surface with talcum powder so that your clay will release easily. If your mold has any deeply indented areas, such as the nose on a face, shape your unbaked clay to fill those areas first (figure 2).

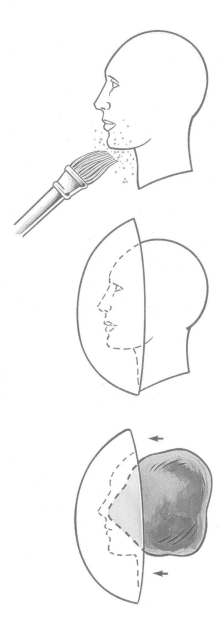

Figure 2

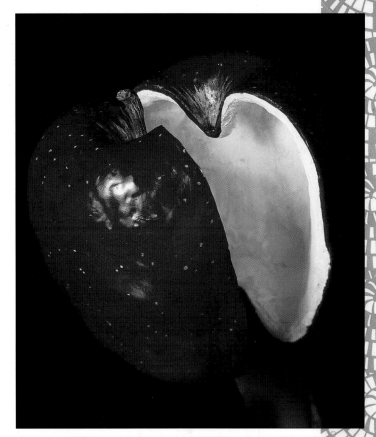

APPLE BOX BY MAGGIE RUDY, APPROX. 3-1/2" x 4" (9 x 10 CM)

MOKUME-GANE

Mokume-gane (literally woodgrain metal) is a traditional Japanese metalworking technique whereby several different metals are laminated into a multi-layered block, then deformed and sanded to reveal interesting patterns. Using a similar process, this can be done with polymer clay too. You can use the process to make a deliberate pattern emerge or to

SUMO FACE PIN AND PRESS MOLD, DONNA KATO, PIN APPROX. 2" x 3-3/4" (5 x 9.5 CM)

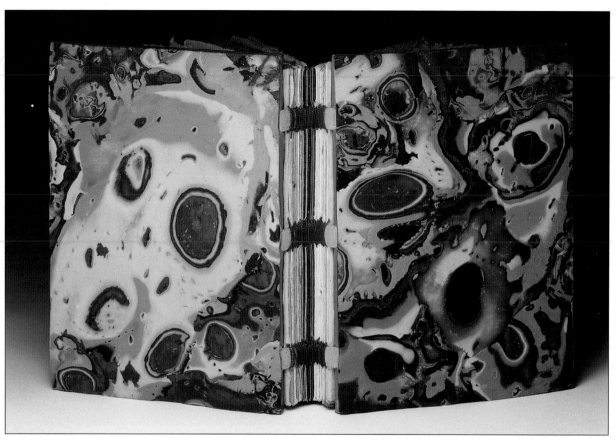

MOKUME-GANE BOOK COVER BY LIZ MACK, APPROX. 4-3/4" x 6-3/4" (12 x 17 CM)

have a random appearance. The mokume-gane in the book cover and frame by Liz Mack looks almost like a geological formation.

To produce this mokume-gane pattern, start with a block of many layers. Then press several pieces of clay onto one side; the shape and size of these pieces will determine your pattern. After turning over the block, press the top surface so that it conforms to the bumps underneath (figure 3). Use a sharp blade to remove thin slices of clay from the high points of the block. This will reveal the lower layers. The slices themselves may be used for decorative elements, and the completed block is useful for any relatively flat object, such as a pin, picture frame, or platter.

If you don't wish to use the clay removed from the top, you can bake the deformed block and sand it to reveal a pattern. Air bubbles can be trapped inside to create an interesting effect. Mokume-gane can be made to look like wood or water, depending on the layering and mix of clay colors.

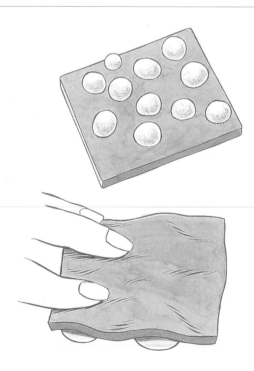

Figure 3

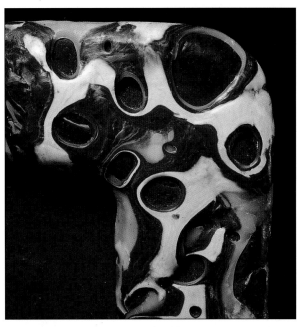

DETAIL, MOKUME-GANE FRAME, LIZ MACK

VENEERS

There are several reasons to use polymer clay in thin layers over a preconstructed form. Sometimes the clay designs are so precious that covering armatures with thin slices is the most efficient use. This is especially true of constructed designs such as mokume-gane and canework. Sometimes, particularly with jewelry and other wearables, weight is a factor.

You can cover almost anything with a veneer of polymer clay. Joanne Hunot uses bright, colorful cane slices to liven up a variety of mundane household objects from salt shakers to screwdrivers. If you have problems with cracks developing, it's probably because the polymer clay and the object being veneered have different coefficients of expansion. This is the rate at which materials expand and contract in reaction to environmental conditions. In most cases, letting the pieces cool down in the oven after they're finished baking will solve the problem.

CANEWORK VENEER APPLIED TO AN ASSORTMENT OF HOUSEHOLD OBJECTS, JOANNE HUNOT

Pier Voulkos creates amazingly lightweight beads by placing a thin veneer of clay over preformed aluminum foil armatures. Because she uses very thin layers of translucent clay, you can see the reflective quality of the aluminum inside. When following this approach, try forming the foil shapes over a metal skewer. Be sure to compress the aluminum foil as much as possible so that the bead doesn't feel soft. Polymer clay adheres best to itself, so try to form a patch, using one or more slices of your pattern, that can be compressed to wrap (and grab) part of the armature.

between two sheets of unprinted newsprint, or you can support and prop the areas prone to sagging. Small wads of tissue paper will not burn at the low baking temperatures required, and these are often sufficient to hold the clay in place until the form is fixed by baking.

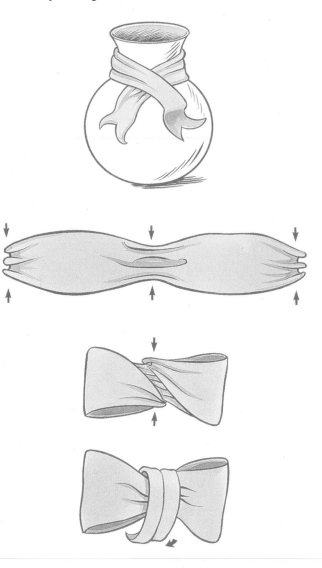

Figure 4

ALUMINUM FOIL ARMATURES AND FINISHED BEAD BY PIER VOULKOS, APPROX. 2-1/4" x 1-3/4" x 3/8" (5.5 x 4.5 x 1 CM)

MODELING SOFT, FLUID SHAPES

The fluidity of polymer clay is deftly exhibited in the soft gold bow on a vase by Donna Kato. For fine modeling of this type, use a clay that is slightly stiff in its raw state and very strong when cured. (Pro-Mat is a good choice.) Modeling a complicated form becomes easier if you reduce it to its component parts. This bow is made in two stages: first the strip that goes around the vase and trails down the front, then the piece that is formed into the loops. Figure 4 shows how this is done.

If the clay is too soft to support the forms you have modeled, you can dry it a little by blotting it

You can model parts or complete figures over aluminum foil or wire that is shaped into wildly eccentric puppet forms with plenty of strength. Mix a variety of test colors for the skin, and bake your samples before choosing a color. The appearance of some skin tones changes noticeably during baking. If you make a solid figure, bake it by bringing up the oven temperature slowly to avoid the shock of sudden heat, which might crack the clay. Hair, eyes, glasses, and other features can be baked into the clay or applied after baking with glue or paint. Fibers that work well for hair include mohair, rayon, and cotton.

DETAIL, VASE WITH RIBBON BOW, BERRIES, AND LEAVES BY DONNA KATO, VASE APPROX. 6" (15 CM) TALL

DOLLS AND OTHER FIGURES

Polymer clay was first invented for doll and puppet crafts. For these applications, it has all the right qualities of color, malleability, translucency, lightness, and durability. Entire figures can be constructed in polymer clay, or you can make just the head and limbs to assemble on a cloth body. When building the complete figure in polymer clay, you can make each part separately, then fit them together and bake again.

If you want to sew the head and limbs to a cloth body, construct the head with a shoulder plate that has a number of holes in it, just as the traditional porcelain dolls were made. To attach the arms and legs, glue a thin strip of leather around the top of each limb so that the leather extends a little beyond the clay (figure 5). Punch a series of holes along the top of the leather strip to make it easier to sew the limb to the body.

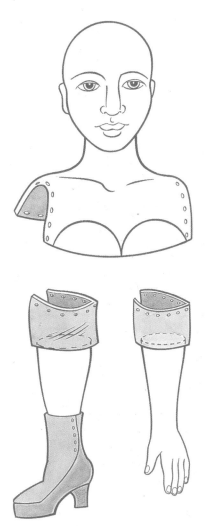

Figure 5

Bon-Bon Bertie, Sarajane Helm, figure approx. 11" (28 cm) tall when standing; photo by Bob Grieser

Detail of *Bon-Bon Bertie*; photo by Bob Grieser

By exploiting various qualities unique to the material, you can build entire scenes like the one created by Sarajane Helm, where nearly every nonfabric object is made of polymer clay. Translucent clays and simple marbling are used for the tabletop and stem of the birdcage. Red clay is modeled to form the box of chocolates and book cover, and tiny snakes of black clay imply the filigree of an ornate birdcage. Gold leaf and metallic powders are liberally applied to embellish the whole scene.

PAINTING WITH POLYMER CLAY

The fanciful illustration done by Claire Laties Davis for a children's poem is dramatically different from her highly realistic portraits (see page 27), but all use a technique akin to painting with clay. Each element of the picture is carved and modeled from slabs of solid-colored clay, then assembled into a low-relief image. To give the surfaces texture and movement, they are manipulated with wood tools. The result looks as if it could have been painted with a palette knife.

In her self portrait (see page 26), Liz Mack takes a slightly different approach to painting with clay. Her colors are partially mixed for a very painterly effect. Although she builds the facial features into a three-dimensional plaque with low relief, you could apply the same technique to a flat image.

POTS, VESSELS, AND RELATED FORMS

Several techniques usually associated with ceramic clay constructions can be applied equally well or better to polymer clay. Pots and related shapes can be coiled, pinched, molded, or slab built. Try two or three different approaches to see which gives you the best results.

Probably the easiest way to shape a vessel is to mold a sheet of clay around an object. Kathleen Dustin used a large rock as the positive shape for her three-legged vessel, and Tory Hughes shaped her footed bowl (see page 33) over a ceiling fixture. Experiment with different objects, but remember to plan for baking and separating the clay from the mold. If you used the inside or outside of a glass bowl to shape your vessel, make sure that the glass is designed to withstand baking temperatures and doesn't have a texture to which the clay might bond. You may wish to dust a thin layer of talcum powder on the glass surface so that the clay will release more easily. Kathleen Dustin used gold leaf as a release agent to remove the clay from the rock.

Slab constructions that aren't shaped by other objects are a bit more challenging but not overly difficult. The main goal is to make sure that your construction doesn't collapse while it bakes or before it has cooled. For square boxes, you can construct cardboard supports for the sides. With other shapes, try gently stuffing paper into areas that are vulnerable. You must keep the clay in these supportive structures until it has fully cooled. If the piece is complex or may collapse while you're building it, construct and bake it in stages.

JUMPING ELEPHANT, CLAIRE LATIES DAVIS, APPROX. 5-1/4" x 5-1/4" (13.5 x 13.5 CM)

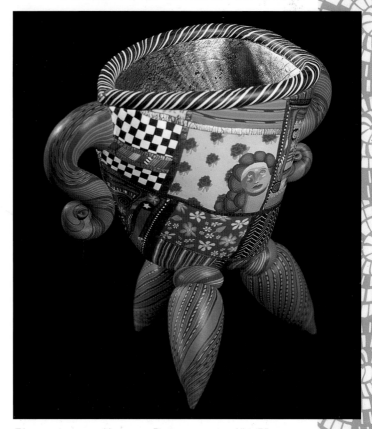

FOOTED VESSEL BY KATHLEEN DUSTIN, APPROX. 6" x 5" x 3-1/4" (15 x 12.5 x 8.5 CM)

VASE, TORY HUGHES, APPROX. 2-1/2" DIA. X 3-1/4" (6.5 X 8.5 CM)

use of slip to ensure bonding between layers, but you should pinch it slightly to obtain full contact.

Tory Hughes used a variation of molding combined with pinching to make her pot. Her method starts with a thick, barrel-shaped bead that is pierced along its axis. This is transformed into a thin-walled

Pinch-pots are shaped entirely by your hands in a slow, satisfying manner that produces very organic shapes. Start with a roughly spherical ball of clay and gently press your thumb into the center to begin to open up the shape. While turning the clay in your hand, continue pinching outward with your thumb (figure 6). Guide the shape of your vessel from the base upwards; a wider shape needs a larger base. As the pot forms in your hand, the walls will become thinner and more delicate. The unavoidable variations in wall thickness and overall shape add charm and character to pinch pots.

To coil a vessel, begin with a long tapered log of clay. Spiral this from the tapered point into a flat disk for the bottom (or cut a circular bottom from a thick sheet of clay). Start the sides by winding another log of clay onto the outer perimeter of the base (figure 7). As the sides of the vessel start to rise, lessen the length of your clay log to maintain better control. Polymer clay doesn't require scoring or the

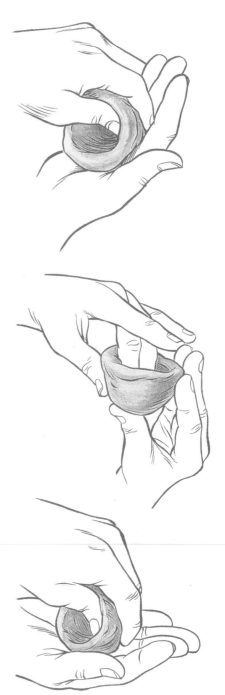

Figure 6

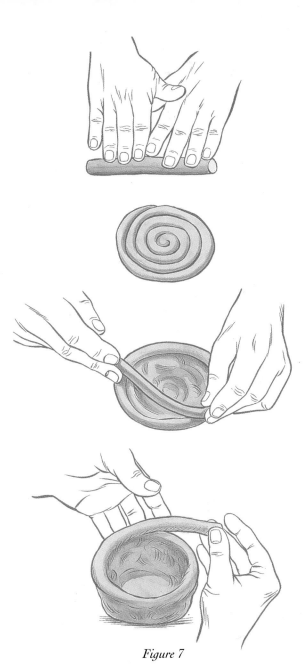

Figure 7

Baking the beads on a wire or skewer allows them to sag into a gentle curve that works very well for necklaces. If you want straight tube beads, bake them in the channels created by folding a piece of rag paper accordion style.

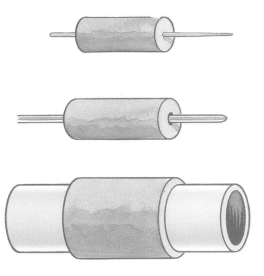

Figure 8

HOLLOW BEADS BY KATHLEEN AMT, AVERAGE APPROX. 2" (5 CM) LONG

cylindrical shape by rolling the bead on progressively larger dowel-shaped tools (figure 8). Once the clay has been opened sufficiently, she uses her fingers to pinch and shape its further construction. The bottom—a flat circle of clay—and mokume-gane embellishments are added later.

Kathleen Amt's hollow beads are made in a similar fashion. Begin with a ball of clay; then pierce it with a needle and work open a hole large enough to insert a small dowel rod. Gently roll the clay-covered dowel to spread the clay to the desired length. Slide the clay tube off the dowel and press two pre-baked disks of clay into the ends, sealing the edges.

EXPERIMENTAL TECHNIQUES

As the use of polymer clay becomes more widespread and more people test its capabilities, new ways of handling the material will constantly be discovered. Two recent experiments by Steven Ford are mentioned here because of the promise they hold for future development. The examples shown are simple, early efforts, but they hint at other possibilities that you might discover for yourself.

The first relates to a casting technique generally applied in metalwork and jewelry making. Called lost wax, it is used in this example to make a simple but unique checkerboard cane. The cane is made by alternating translucent polymer clay with bee's wax. When the slices cut from the cane are baked, the wax melts out and leaves behind voids that would be nearly impossible to obtain in any other way. During baking, an absorbent surface such as a paper towel is used to collect the wax as it melts.

The second set of examples shows some of the effects that can be achieved by turning polymer clay on a lathe designed for wood. The clay pieces were intentionally underbaked, both in time and temperature, to make the cutting easier. The pieces were turned on the lathe by Michael Mode, a master wood turner, and demonstrate a sampling of the remarkable shapes that can be obtained using this method. The polymer clay holds extraordinary detail and has the added benefits of infinite color combinations, calculated designs, and no knots or grain to fight. After the pieces were finished on the lathe, they were rebaked to fully cure the clay.

CANE (UNBAKED) AND SLICES (BAKED) MADE USING LOST WAX TECHNIQUE, STEVEN FORD, APPROX. 3/4" x 3/4" (2 x 2 CM) IN CROSS SECTION

EXAMPLES OF POLYMER CLAY BY STEVEN FORD, TURNED ON A WOOD LATHE BY MICHAEL MODE, LARGEST APPROX. 4" (10 CM) LONG

ithout a doubt, the single most popular method for working with polymer clay is caning. This technique is based on the Venetian glassmaking process called *millefiori*, in which a selection of colored glass rods are bundled together to create a design. Each slice cut from the end of the bundle, which is called a cane, reveals the same pattern. Canes made from polymer clay are considerably easier to work with than those made with molten glass, and the design possibilities are virtually unlimited.

Like glass, polymer clay can be drawn out to reduce the overall diameter of the cane. This characteristic more than any other helps explain the seduction of canework. Any pattern, whether simple or complex, can be made into a neatly formed miniature.

When first learning to make canes, one concept to become accustomed to is the necessity to think in both two and three dimensions simultaneously. Canes are equally valued for their two-dimensional images in cross section and for the multiple copies made possible by their three-dimensional construc-

PIN BY SUSAN PERRY AND BILL GUNDLING, APPROX. 3" X 1-1/2" (7.5 x 4 CM)

tion. Start simply with spirals and checkerboards until this concept feels comfortable.

There are very few secrets to mastering this technique. The first is to practice making the basic forms until you can produce them consistently and flaw-

BEADS BY SAM TERRY AND DAVE ALLENDER, APPROX. 1" (2.5 CM)

1

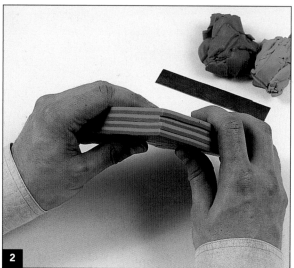

2

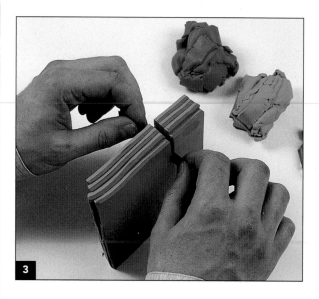

3

lessly. Second, plan your designs before attempting to make them; color sketches are sometimes useful. Finally, make sure that all of the components of your cane are equally warm and conditioned to the same consistency.

Proficiency in technique will soon evolve into your own individual style. For examples of two very different styles, look at the pin and assortment of beads pictured on the previous page. The canework in the pin by Susan Perry and Bill Gundling shows a high degree of control, and their design reflects a strong Asian influence. (This piece features caned polymer clay inlaid in wood; the two different surfaces are unified with a single water-based finish.) In contrast, Sam Terry and Dave Allender achieve beautiful painterly effects using complex but fairly casual constructions. Some of their beads show the mottled colors that result from partially kneading clay that has been mixed in a food processor.

GEOMETRIC PATTERNS

A good place to begin making canes is with simple geometric patterns. These use basic forms, such as sheets of clay, that are assembled, cut, and reassembled into more complicated designs. Because of their regularity, you can see immediately if you go astray during construction. Geometric patterns are also quite versatile; just by cutting and reassembling the components in different ways, a single basic pattern such as a striped loaf can create a variety of designs.

Try this for yourself. Mix two colors of clay and condition them by hand or machine, as described in the chapter on getting started. Using a roller or pasta machine, flatten each color into a rectangular sheet. Stack the two sheets, and if one is larger than the other, place the smaller sheet on top. Trim the edges, cutting through both, so that you have one long rectangle with regular dimensions (photo 1).

Cut the rectangle into quarters and stack the pieces to form a block of stripes with alternating colors (photo 2). Standing the block on end, cut off a well-proportioned rectangular segment (photo 3). Save the rest of the striped loaf for other projects.

Now cut the rectangular block from corner to corner, top to bottom, as straight as possible (photo 4). This step might take some practice, but you'll find that cutting vertically gives you more control with the blade.

You can reassemble the resulting triangles in two ways to form a parallelogram; either join the striped edges (photo 5) or lay the two solid-colored sides together (photo 6). The latter approach results in a parallelogram with diagonal stripes. To convert this to a rectangle, cut two small triangular shapes off the sides (photo 7).

Compress but don't stretch the diagonally striped rectangular cane from one end to the other to work out any air bubbles and adhere the many layers into one piece of clay (photo 8). Start to "cane out" (reduce) the compressed block by gently tugging on one end with one hand while you simultaneously

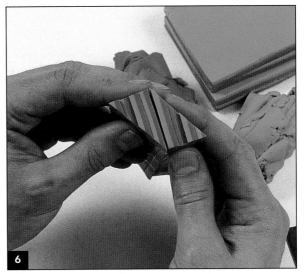

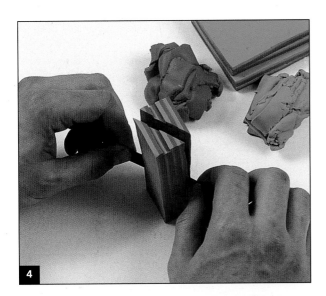

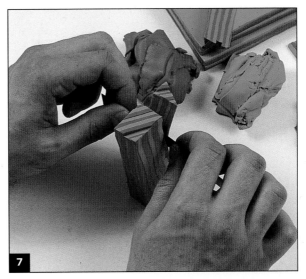

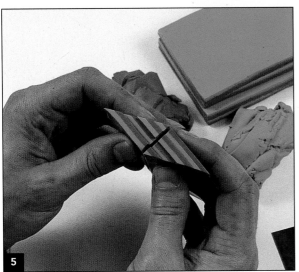

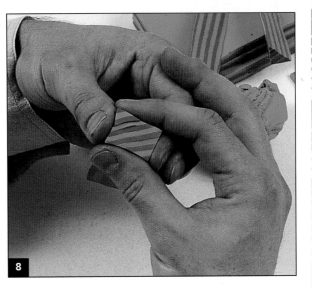

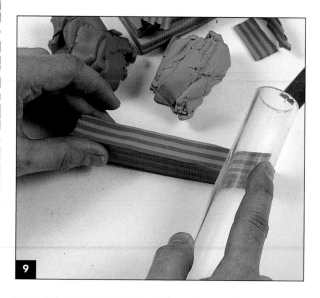

roll lightly with a roller held in your other hand (photo 9). This motion should be a single gesture and will take some practice getting used to, but it is fundamental to reducing square designs with maximum control.

An alternative to reducing the cane with a roller is to use the flat part of your fingers to burnish the surface as you tug the cane with the fingers of your other hand (photo 10). This technique is especially good for repairing any cracks or tears that might develop on the surface of the cane.

Move your hands up and down the length of the cane as needed to elongate it evenly and to prevent the ends from becoming too distorted. Some distortion of the ends is inevitable; your goal is to maximize the amount of usable cane (photo 11).

With the cane elongated, trim off the distortions on the ends until you see a clear design (photo 12). Find the middle of the cane by putting the two ends together; then cut it in half. Reassemble the two halves by placing them together lengthwise, working from one end to the other to eliminate air bubbles (photo 13). This assembly creates a mirror image of the angled lines.

Repeat the reduction with the roller or your fingers until you're satisfied with the scale of the design

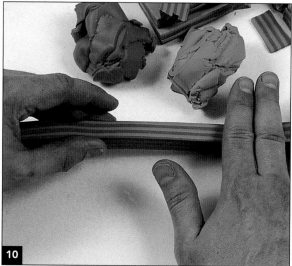

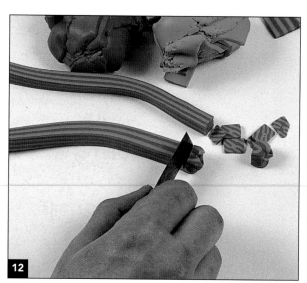

(photo 14). Trim the ends, cut in half, and reassemble again (photo 15).

To make simple cylindrical beads with a veneer of cane design, cut and join two slices of your cane pattern (photo 16). Then roll a cylindrical core of polymer clay and cut it to match the width of the joined slice (photo 17). Wrap the slice around the core, working the seam together with your fingers

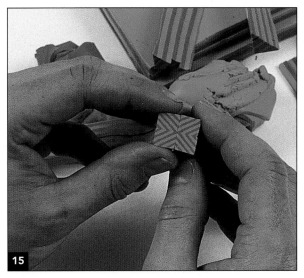

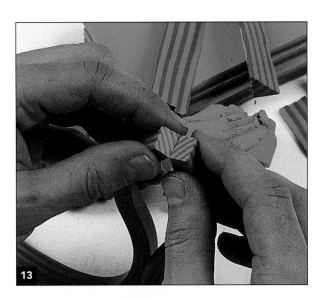

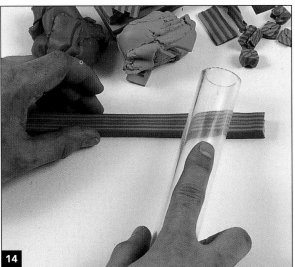

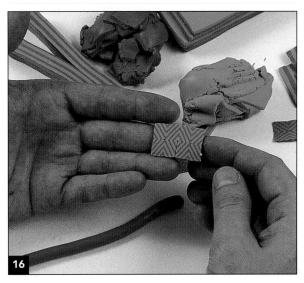

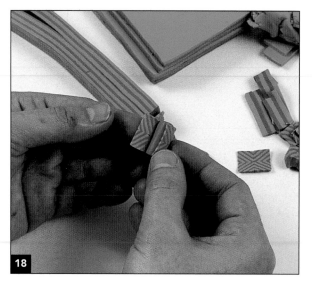

18

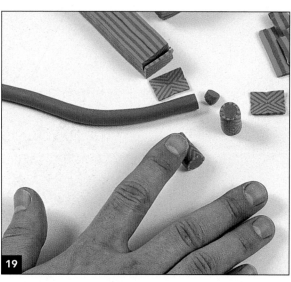

19

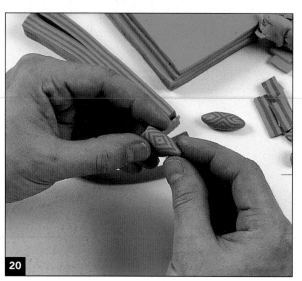

20

(photo 18). Gently roll the bead to smooth the surface (photo 19). If desired, taper the ends to rounded points (photo 20).

Stacking sheets of clay into striped loaves is the basis for many other designs as well. One of the simplest is the jelly roll. Using rectangular sheets in two or more colors, place one on top of another with the ends slightly staggered. Lightly flatten the leading edge; then roll the stripes into a tight spiral (see figure 1).

Another simple possibility is the checkerboard. Start with as many layers of alternating colors as you want squares of color (e.g., a four-layered block will make a four-by-four checkerboard). Setting the

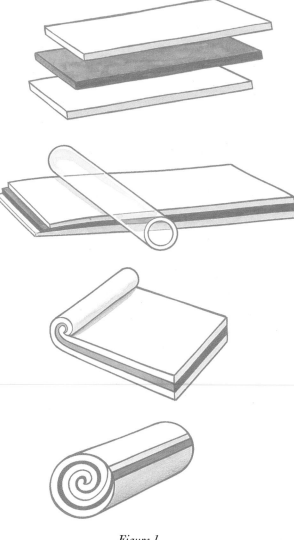

Figure 1

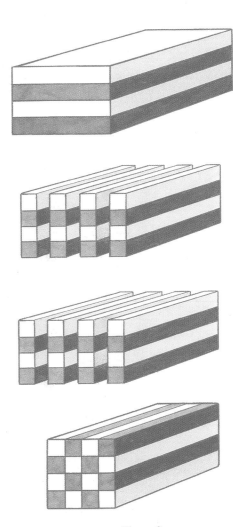

Figure 2

MONA LISA BEAD BY CHERI PYLES, APPROX. 1" (2.5 CM)

Although Liz Mack's portrait isn't really a cane, it illustrates one way to build a cane of an organic image. Logs of various colors and sizes are put together with slab forms to create a loosely rendered picture. This technique is similar to the way the impressionist painters of the 19th century used dabs of paint to describe forms. Cheri Pyles' Mona Lisa bead is an example of a face cane that has been reduced.

striped loaf on end, cut lengthwise slices that are equal in thickness to one striped layer. Reassemble the slices by turning over every other one to produce the checkerboard (figure 2).

ORGANIC DESIGNS

Natural images are looser and more forgiving than geometric ones, but they are often more complex and require more planning. Whereas geometric patterns demand precise assemblies of simple elements, organic designs are more like jigsaw puzzles put together with three-dimensional pieces. Construct the components first; then assemble them into the desired image.

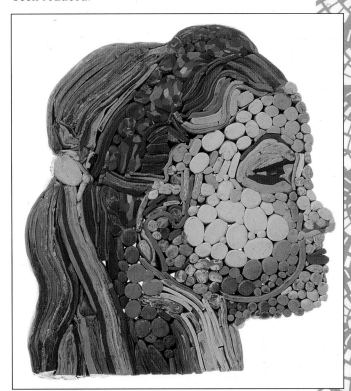

PORTRAIT BY LIZ MACK, APPROX. 5-1/2" x 6" (14 x 15 CM)

One example of an organic design is a butterfly cane. Because a butterfly is symmetrical, you can build a cane consisting of one wing and half the body, then cut two slices and join them down the middle. (The same approach can be taken with any other symmetrical cane design, including a face or figure.)

To get started, mix a range of colors for the majority of the wing (photo 21). By mixing a variety of tones, you can imitate the fibrous texture of actual butterfly wings. Flatten these into sheets about 1/8" (3 mm) thick (or use the widest setting on a pasta machine). Also mix some black clay and flatten it as thin as possible (use the thinnest setting). Finally, mix two bright but related colors for the wing spots and a small amount of brown and black for the body.

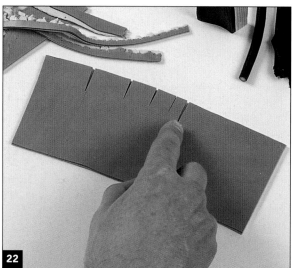

Begin the upper wing by stacking two contrasting sheets of clay together and cutting the stack into strips of various widths (photo 22). Assemble these pieces into a wedge shape by aligning all of the cut sides on one edge and stepping down to a single strip on the other (photo 23). Then pinch the layers into a solid wedge (photo 24). Don't worry about distortions; they will give the wing a fluid, natural appearance.

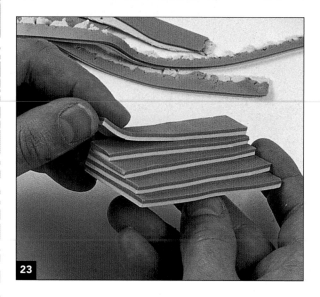

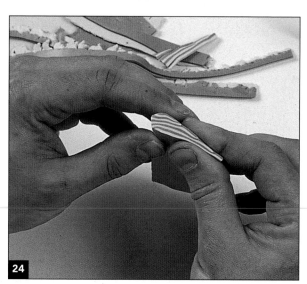

Add more layers by roughly tearing strips from the remaining sheets and laying them onto the long sides of the wedge (photos 25 and 26). Be careful not to trap air bubbles between these layers because they can cause holes later. When you're satisfied with your additions, wrap the wedge in a sheet of very thin black clay (photo 27). This will appear as the vein in the butterfly's wing.

Compress and gently stretch the wedge until it is four or five times its original length (photo 28). Then cut this long cane into several pieces (photo 29). You can make all of the pieces the same length, or you can build more variety into the repeat of this

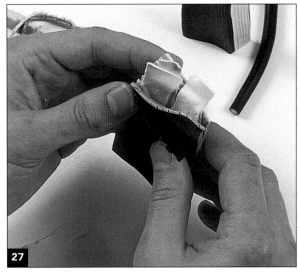

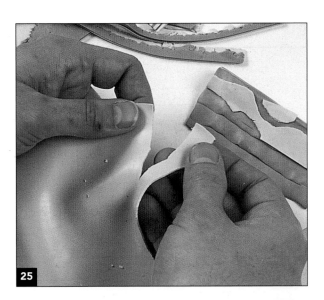

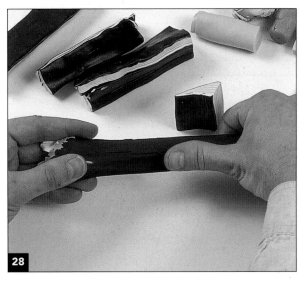

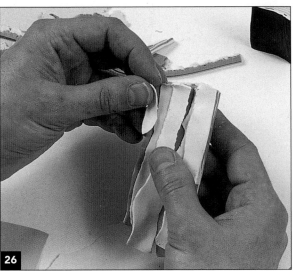

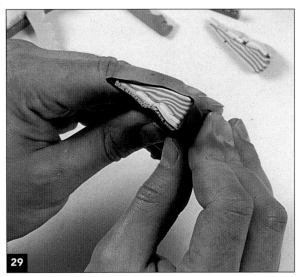

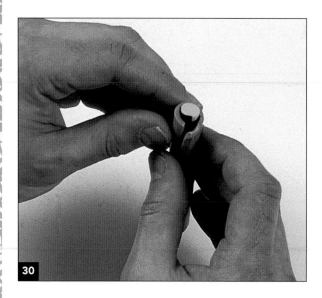

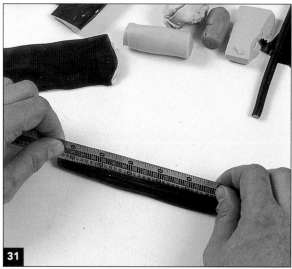

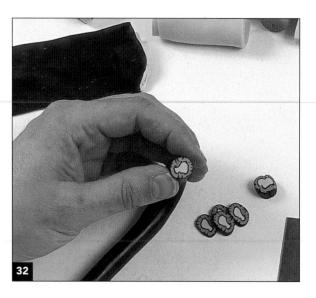

wedge shape by cutting some shorter. Stretch the shorter pieces out to the same length as the others to obtain the same pattern in a variety of sizes. Finally, trim the distorted ends off so that you can see what you have made.

To create a spot for the wing, make a typical bull's eye. Start by rolling out a small log of brightly colored clay. Then flatten a thin sheet of black clay and cut a straight edge along one side. Wrap the clay around the log and cut another straight edge to make a butt joint. After smoothing the joint, add a thicker layer of the other, related color, then a final layer of thin black clay (photo 30).

Using a blunt-edged tool such as a ruler, roughly press deep ridges into the outside surface of the bull's eye (photo 31). This distorts the concentric layers of color and makes a spot with a fibrous texture. Then roll the log smooth again (photo 32).

Assemble the wedges that you've created and position the spot cane wherever you want (photo 33). For a realistic design, refer to pictures of real butterflies to understand where the spots should go.

Repeat the same process for making the lower wing lobe (photos 34 and 35). Some natural species have very different colors for the upper and lower wings. This is an opportunity to add more color variety to

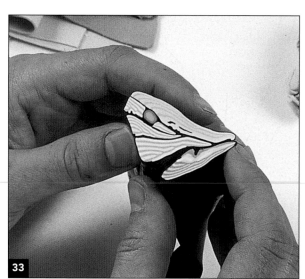

the design, but be consistent with the process so that the result looks unified. Join the top and bottom wings, adding small sheets of clay to anchor any spots along the outer edges (photos 36 and 37).

To create the impression of a butterfly body, add strips of black and brown clay to the middle axis of the design (photo 38). Remember, this will double in thickness when the two halves are assembled, so don't make it too wide.

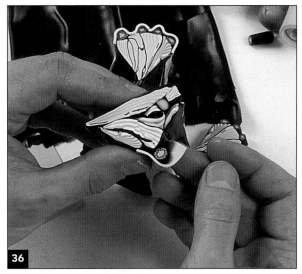

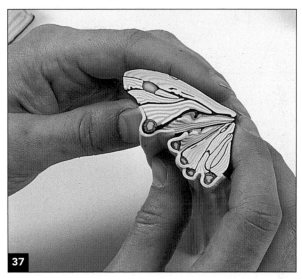

Before cutting thin slices from your completed half-butterfly, allow the warm and well-handled cane to cool and stiffen. Then join two slices together at the body by pinching the seam with your fingers (photos 39 and 40).

39

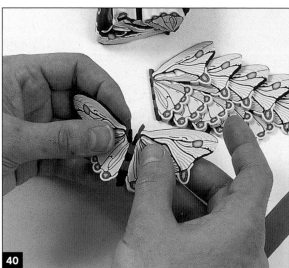

40

When making a butterfly cane, all of the reduction is done during the construction of the individual components, not after the cane is finished. Canes with uneven shapes such as this are difficult, if not impossible, to reduce without causing unwanted distortions. For that reason, many artists build their complex canes into shapes that can be handled more easily. This requires "filling in the blanks" around the outer edges of your design.

One simple example of this is a star cane. The main components of the star are a cylindrical log

and five triangular ones. After assembling these into the characteristic star shape, you must make five additional triangular logs in another, background color. A thin sheet of clay applied as an outer layer provides additional stability and an attractive border. As shown in figure 3, this makes a cylindrical cane that is easy to reduce to any size needed for your project.

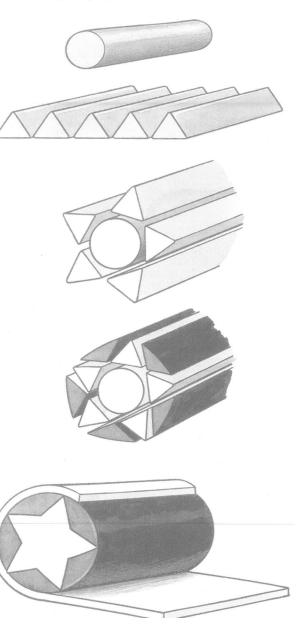

Figure 3

PROJECTS

DANCING FIGURES NECKLACE

A HINT OF SILVER IMPLIES FORMALITY, BUT THESE DANCING FIGURES
ARE APPROPRIATE FOR ANY OCCASION.

YOU WILL NEED

About 6 oz. (170 g) of scrap clay, one or more patterned canes, blade, piercing tool, 2" (5-cm) head pins, 20-gauge silver wire, jump rings, accent beads, small silver beads, chain-nose or needle-nose pliers

MAKING THE FIGURES

1. Form the heads by making 1/2"-diameter (1.5-cm) balls of scrap clay and covering them with thin slices from one or more patterned canes.

2. For the arms and legs, make a long clay log 1/4" (6 mm) in diameter and cover the outside of the log with slices from your canes. Cut the covered log into 1" (2.5-cm) pieces and bend the pieces to make several sets of arms and legs.

3. Cut shorter lengths, about 1/2" (1.5 cm) long, from the cane-covered log to make beads for the necklace links.

3. Pierce all of the beads and bake them according to the manufacturer's directions. For best results, suspend the beads on a wire while baking.

ASSEMBLY

1. To make each figure, stack three beads onto a head pin, placing the legs on the bottom, then arms and head. Using the pliers, make a loop at the top of the pin and wrap the end of the wire around a few times to secure it (figure 1).

2. Make the necklace links by placing one polymer bead, two accent beads, and two silver beads on a piece of wire. Using the pliers, make a loop on each end (figure 2).

3. Assemble the necklace by using jump rings to join the links and adding a dancing figure wherever desired.

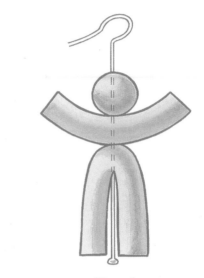

Figure 1

Figure 2

Design: TAMELA WELLS LAITY
Size: 27" (68.5 CM) LONG

71

BUTTONS

LIGHTWEIGHT, COLORFUL, AND DURABLE CUSTOMIZED BUTTONS ARE A GREAT WAY TO EXPRESS YOUR INDIVIDUALITY—AND EXPERIMENT WITH NEW TECHNIQUES.

Design: STEVEN FORD AND DAVID FORLANO
Sizes: FROM 3/4" (2 CM) TO 1-3/4" (4.5 CM) DIAMETER

YOU WILL NEED

Small amounts of polymer clay, cane slices or molded forms, piercing tool, button findings, cyanoacrylate glue

MAKING BUTTONS

1. The easiest way to make a polymer clay button is to cut a slice about 1/8" (3 mm) thick from one of your canes. Then poke two holes in the center. The space between them is the weakest point of the button, so don't place the holes too close together. The small button shown in the middle of the photograph is a slight variation of this approach; it features two intersecting slices.

2. If you don't like the holes to be visible, you can also make buttons by gluing button cover findings or clear plastic button shanks onto the backs of cane slices, molded forms, or other clay shapes that are flat on the back. For extra durability, reinforce the cane slice or decorative piece with a layer of one of the stronger baking clays (such as Cernit).

3. Another approach is to apply a veneer of clay over a commercially available metal dome finding (the type commonly used for making fabric-covered buttons). When applying the clay to this type of finding, be sure to continue coverage onto the back of the finding to ensure good adhesion. One variation here shows a swirl pattern made with a tiny log embellished with metallic leaf. You can also decorate the outer edges with colorful canes.

4. Bake the buttons according to the instructions given by the clay manufacturer.

5. If you dry clean the garment, cover the polymer clay buttons with plastic wrap and aluminum foil to protect them from chemical damage. On garments that are hand washed, use a mild soap and warm or cold water.

AUTUMN LEAVES NECKLACE

VARIATIONS OF THE SAME CANE DESIGN, MADE WITH A TOTAL OF
FOUR TO SIX AUTUMN COLORS, PRODUCE A MEDLEY OF LEAVES
WORTHY OF NATURE HERSELF. FOR A VARIATION, TRY USING MOTTLED
COLORS OF CLAY TO ADD TEXTURE TO THE LEAVES.

Design: ELISE WINTERS
Sizes: NECKLACE, 22" (56 CM) LONG;
PENDANT, 2" x 2" (5 x 5 CM); EARRINGS, 2" (5 CM) LONG

Autumn Leaves Necklace

■

You Will Need

About 2-1/2 oz. (71 g)* of each color (three per leaf cane) of polymer clay, pasta machine or roller, blade, darning needle, beading cord, clasp, rayon cord (for pendant), earring clips or posts

* This amount of polymer clay makes enough leaves for two or three necklaces.

Basic Leaf Cane

1. After conditioning the clay, flatten each color—gold, off white, and rust—into a sheet. Start with the rust; then make the white sheet twice as thick and the gold sheet three times as thick. This is a breeze with a pasta machine: use setting #5 for the rust, #3 for the off white, and #1 for the gold.

2. Make two 2" x 3" (5 x 7.5 cm) striped blocks, each with one layer of off white placed between two layers of rust (figure 1). Set these aside to use for the center veins.

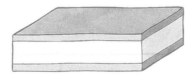

Figure 1

3. Then make a striped block approximately 3" x 5" (7.5 x 12.5 cm) with gold at the bottom, followed by rust, off white, and rust. Cut and stack the block twice to make a 3" x 1-1/4" (7.5 x 3 cm) cane. Then add a layer of gold to the top (figure 2).

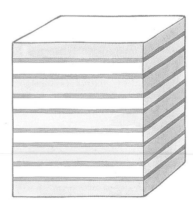

Figure 2

4. Compress the cane so that the cross section is nearly square. Then stand the striped cane on end and cut diagonally down through it.

5. Flip one side of the cane so that the stripes now meet at a right angle. In the diagonal space in the

center, insert one of the reserved center veins from step 2 (figure 3). Gently trim off the excess vein and press the components together into a single cane.

6. With the cane standing on end, slice down on both sides to remove the corners (figure 4).

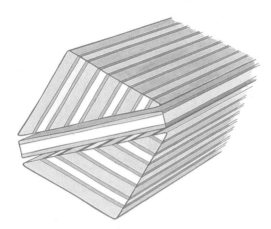

Figure 3

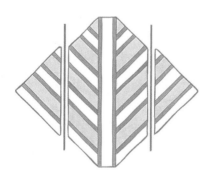

Figure 4

7. Make a smaller version of the leaf cane by putting the second center vein from step 2 between the two corner sections. Then trim the corners of the smaller cane to match the larger one.

8. Gently pinch and roll both canes to form them into rounded leaf shapes. Then stretch and pull them gradually to reduce them to the sizes desired.

9. To make beads, cut slices 3/16" (5 mm) thick and pierce them through the edges with a darning needle. Apply thin slices of the canes to a heart-shaped pendant or to strips of gold clay folded into knots for earrings.

10. Bake the pieces according to the clay manufacturer's recommendations. When they're cool, string the beads on beading cord and attach a clasp (figure 5).

Figure 5

MEMORY WIRE BRACELETS

SLEEK AND SOPHISTICATED, THESE OUT-OF-THE-ORDINARY BRACELETS
DERIVE THEIR FORM FROM MEMORY WIRE, WHICH COILS LIKE A SPRING
AROUND YOUR WRIST.

YOU WILL NEED

A total of about 2-1/2 oz. (71 g) of polymer clay in two or more colors plus translucent, assortment of canes, roller, blade, four 9" (23-cm) lengths of 16-gauge rigid wire, 33" (84-cm) length of memory wire, sheet of paper, needle-nose pliers, commercial beads (optional)

MAKING BEADS

1. Make the tube beads using very flexible clay; one approach is to mix equal amounts of translucent clay with one or more colors. Whether you use striped canes or solid colors, make sure that all of the clay has the same consistency.

2. To make a tube, roll a 1/2"-square (1.5-cm) cane slice or piece of clay into a cylinder 1" (2.5 cm) long. Pierce and thread the cylinder onto one length of the rigid wire as you would for a bead. With the clay still on the wire, use a zigzag rolling movement with your fingers to elongate the clay on the wire.

3. As the tube gets longer, the center hole will grow larger. Squeeze the ends of the tube around the wire and gently twist and stretch the tube bit by bit until it is snug around the wire again. Continue rolling and elongating until the tube is about 3/16" (5 mm) in diameter and 6-8" (15-20 cm) long.

4. Following the same process, make three more tubes. You will need about 21-24" (53-61 cm) in tube beads.

5. Use the remaining clay and canes to make an assortment of beads and other objects in various sizes.

6. Bake all of the beads on wires, following the recommendations of the clay manufacturer.

ASSEMBLY

1. An easy way to arrange your beads is to fold a piece of paper accordion style so that you can line up your beads in the troughs (figure 1). If the paper is folded so that each trough is 9" (23 cm) long, you'll use about 3-1/2 troughs to fill your bracelet. Assemble a pleasing arrangement of beads and tubes in the troughs.

2. Using the pliers, make a loop at one end of the memory wire. Then use your fingers to straighten the last inch (2.5 cm) or so of the other end of the wire.

3. Thread the beads and tubes onto the wire, checking the arrangement before adding the next row of beads. Adjust your arrangement or add spacers as necessary to hide the wire as it coils.

4. When the arrangement is complete, cut the wire with 1/2" (1.5 cm) to spare at the end. Bend this into a loop using the pliers. Add small charms or beads to the loops at the ends if desired. Then gently bend the bracelet into consistent circles.

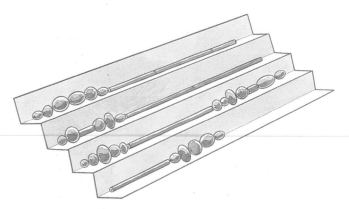

Figure 1

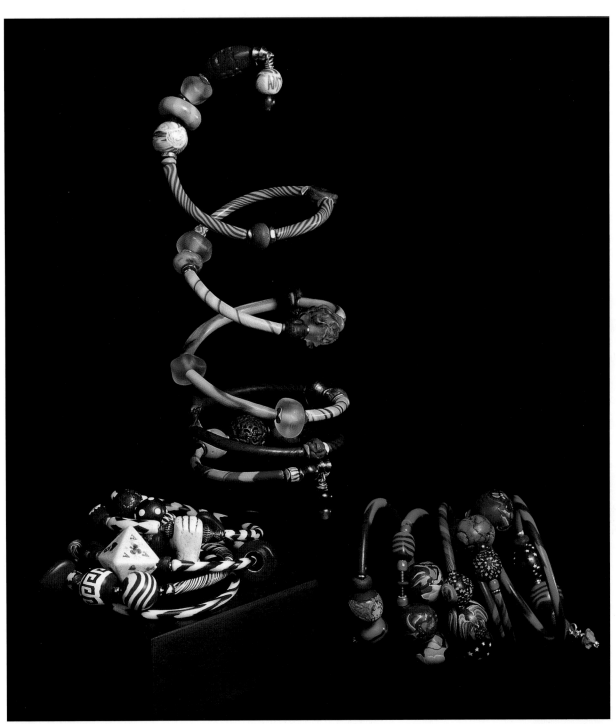

Design: KATHLEEN AMT
Size: APPROXIMATELY 2-1/2" (6.5 CM) DIAMETER

Navajo Eye-Dazzler Beads

One of the most popular of the basic Navajo patterns is the eye-dazzler; its brilliant geometric pattern can be achieved by joining two identical canes that are made in complementary colors.

■

Design: Z KRIPKE
Sizes: FROM 1/2" x 3/4" (1.5 x 2 CM) TO 1-1/4" x 1-1/2" (3 x 4 CM)

You Will Need

About 1/2 oz. (14 g) of color A, 1-1/2 oz. (42 g) of color B, 2-1/2 oz. (71 g) of color C, 3-1/2 oz. (99 g) of color D, 4-1/2 oz. (127 g) of color E, 5-1/2 oz. (156 g) of color F (for each of two canes; see figures 1-3 for color placement), roller, blade

Making the Canes

1. For the center element, make one square log of color A and three square logs of color B. Standing the color A log on end, cut it in half diagonally. Repeat with one of the color B logs. Reassemble the halves to make two new bicolored logs and arrange the four logs so that color A makes an hourglass pattern in the center (figure 1). Note: All square logs should be exactly equal in size throughout the construction of the cane.

2. Now make two solid square logs of color D and 10 square logs that are diagonally halved using colors C and D. Arrange these around the central element, placing the solid-colored logs at 3 o'clock and 9 o'clock, as shown in figure 2.

3. Add another frame using 18 diagonally divided logs made of colors E and F and two solid logs of color F (figure 3).

4. If desired, add a thin sheet of clay around the entire cane to give some separation between this pattern and that of the secondary cane.

5. Following the same process, make a second cane in colors that coordinate well with the first one.

Assembling the Pattern

1. Cut both canes into two segments of equal length. Standing one segment of the secondary cane (the one you want to be less prominent in the design) on end, cut it in half diagonally. Cut the other segment of the same cane into quarters (figure 4).

2. Assemble the canes into the pattern shown in figure 5 and, if desired, wrap the completed cane with a thin sheet of clay.

3. Thick slices (about 3/16" or 5 mm) cut from this cane make stunning beads, and thin slices add drama and color to other projects.

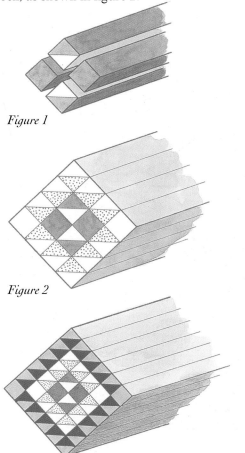

Figure 1

Figure 2

Figure 3

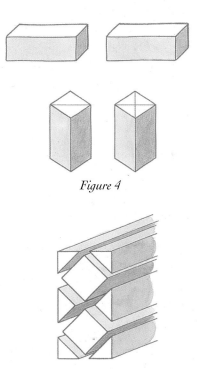

Figure 4

Figure 5

MOSAIC EARRINGS

THESE OPULENT EARRINGS ARE SO CONVINCING THAT YOUR FRIENDS
WON'T BELIEVE THEY'RE NOT MADE OF REAL TURQUOISE, SHELL, AND JET.

■

Design: CAROLYN POTTER
Size: 1/2" x 2-1/4" (1.5 x 5.5 CM)

YOU WILL NEED

About 1-1/2 oz. (42 g) of black, 1/2 oz. (14 g) or less of orange, red, mint, light turquoise, apricot, light blue, and terra-cotta polymer clay, clay conditioner, roller, blade, 280-, 400-, and 600-grit wet/dry sandpaper, 00 steel wool, electric drill, silver wire, chain-nose pliers, two silver shepherd's hook findings

IMITATION CORAL SHELL

1. Blend the dark red-orange shell color by mixing equal amounts of red and apricot clay with double that amount of orange.

2. Pinch, don't roll, the resulting red-orange clay, some unmixed orange clay, and a small amount of apricot clay into three separate sheets, each about 1" x 2" (2.5 x 5 cm). Pinching the sheets makes them uneven and more natural in appearance. They should have different thicknesses, and the apricot sheet should be much thinner than the other colors.

3. Stack the layers; then cut the resulting loaf in half. Alternating the colors, stack the two halves. Now pinch and elongate the striped block to twice its length. Repeat this process a total of five times.

5. Cut one or two slices, each 1/8" (3 mm) thick.

FAUX TURQUOISE

1. Mix equal amounts of light turquoise and mint to make a light teal-colored clay.

2. Flatten the light teal, some light turquoise, and some light blue clay into three separate sheets, each 1/8" (3 mm) thick.

JET

1. Flatten a portion of the black clay into a sheet 1/8" (3 mm) thick.

ASSEMBLY

1. Flatten the remaining black clay into a sheet 1/8" (3 mm) thick and cut two shapes for the earring bases. If you want them to be identical, use the first piece as a pattern to cut the second.

2. Using the blade, cut narrow strips about 1/4" (6 mm) wide from each of the faux materials, cutting across the stripes in the coral shell pattern. Then slice off the small pieces needed to make the design. Vary the sizes and shapes to create a more natural appearance.

3. Leaving small spaces between the pieces, assemble the design onto the earring bases. Gently press the tiny pieces onto the bases to adhere the clay together.

4. Bake these as recommended by the clay manufacturer.

5. Mix a dark brown clay (adding a touch of black to the terra-cotta) and soften it with clay conditioner to make a grout for your mosaic. If the brown is lighter than the black used for the jet, the separation between the black pieces will show in the finished work (a desired effect).

6. Using your fingers and a narrow tool, force the grout into the spaces between the tiles. Leave a thin layer (nearly translucent) on the pattern pieces. This keeps the grout from pulling out.

7. Bake again as directed.

8. Sand away the excess grout to reveal the inlay effect, smooth the sides, and round off the corners. Begin with the coarsest paper and progress to the finest. Then polish the sanded work with the steel wool.

ADDING THE FINDINGS

1. Using a fine bit, drill a hole at the top of each earring.

2. Thread a piece of silver wire through the hole in one earring and make an oval shape; then wrap the wire around itself in the center of the oval (figure 1). Repeat with the other earring. Attach the shepherd's hook findings to complete both earrings.

Figure 1

CROCODILE TILE

DESIGNS MADE BY IMPRESSING A FIGURE INTO SOFT CLAY ARE ESPE-
CIALLY WELL SUITED TO FLAT OBJECTS, SUCH AS THIS DECORATIVE TILE.

YOU WILL NEED

About 4 oz. (113 g) of black clay, pencil,
paper, craft knife, pasta machine or roller,
ruler, pot scrubber or other textured surface, 6" x 6" (15 x 15 cm) ceramic floor tile
or square sheet of strong polymer clay,
verdigris and copper rubbing compounds,
cyanoacrylate glue (if ceramic tile is used)

MAKING THE STAMP

1. Sketch a design on a piece of paper; then use this
as a pattern to cut your design from a smoothly
rolled piece of scrap clay. If desired, embellish the
stamp with texture and designs. For this tile, the
artist made two crocodile stamps and pulled the
mouth open on one.

2. Bake as directed by the clay manufacturer.

3. To make the stamp easier to use, a knob may be
glued to the back.

THE TILE

1. Roll the black clay to an even thickness of about
1/8" (3 mm) or use the #1 setting on a pasta machine.
Then cut the clay into nine 2" (5-cm) squares.

2. Using the pot scrubber or other tool, texture the
tiles to give the clay a slightly pitted appearance.
Then press your stamp(s) onto the surface.

3. Bake, following the manufacturer's recommendations.

4. Arrange the cooled pieces on the floor tile (or on
a flat, smooth sheet of polymer clay). Make thin logs
of black clay to use for mortar and press these
between the baked tiles.

5. Strongly texture the mortar and bake the assembly. If your underlying tile is polymer, then you can
bake the two together to adhere them. If you use a
ceramic floor tile, then you must glue the two
together after the polymer has cooled.

6. Finish the piece, including the edges, with the
rubbing compounds.

Design: ANNA RIDDILE
Size: 6" x 6" (15 x 15 CM)

BEADED BASKETS

IF YOU LOVE TO MAKE BEADS, A BEADED BASKET OFFERS NEW
CHALLENGES FOR MIXING AND MATCHING COLORS AND PATTERNS ON
A LARGE SCALE.

■

YOU WILL NEED

Total of about 27-1/2 to 32 oz. (778-905 g)
of polymer clay in assorted colors, 13-1/2 to
18-1/2 oz. (390-520 g) of scrap clay, piercing tool or electric drill, 5 yds. (.5 m) of 3-
mm bonsai wire*, 10 yds. (1 m) of 2.5-mm
bonsai wire, cyanoacrylate glue, automobile
touch-up paint

*Bonsai wire is anodized aluminum wire
that is used to train bonsai plants. It is thick,
yet pliable enough to be twisted into shape
with your hands. It comes in several dark
metallic colors and coordinates well with
beads that are embellished with copper,
bronze, or gold leaf.

BEADS

1. Create an assortment of beads in a variety of
shapes, sizes, and patterns. The larger (blue) basket
contains 220 round beads, ranging in size from
about 3/8" (1 cm) to 3/4" (2 cm) in diameter. There
are also 80 cut cylinder beads and 64 disk beads.
Pierce or drill all of the beads with holes slightly
larger than the 3-mm wire.

2. To construct the basket, you'll need about 48 temporary spacer beads. These will be discarded, so
make them from scrap clay. Form a log about 1/2"
(1.5 cm) in diameter and cut cylinder beads 3/8" (1
cm) long. Then cut out a wedge from each so that the
bead can be slipped on and off the wire (figure 1).

Figure 1

ASSEMBLING THE BASKET

1. The basket is built from the rim down by creating
a series of rings in graduated sizes and connecting
them together. The top ring of the larger basket is 34"
(about 86 cm) in circumference, which is divided into
eight design segments. The vertical connectors
between rings are placed between the segments.
Once you've arranged the beads you wish to place on
the top ring, thread them onto the wire and place a
spacer at the end of each segment. Then glue the two
ends of the wire together inside a medium-sized bead.

2. For every subsequent ring, assemble each series
of beads as needed. The size and number of beads
you choose will determine the circumference of each
ring, but you can estimate it by subtracting 1-1/2" (4
cm) from the length of the previous ring. Before you
cut the wire, hold the ring in place to see if you like
the shape.

3. Make the second ring the same way you did the
first, but place a spacer at the center and end of
each segment. Eight spacers accommodate the connectors to the top ring and eight provide for connec-
tions to the ring below.

4. When the first two rings are finished, cut eight 8"
(20.5-cm) lengths of 2.5-mm wire for connectors.
Slip a spacer off the top ring and wrap one end of a
piece of wire three times around the ring where the
spacer was (figure 2). Wrap the wire tightly; then
snip the residual end and pinch it down with pliers.
After some practice, you will be able to make very
even "knots" that all face the same direction.
Automobile touch-up paint can be used to cover
small scratches and the bright metal ends of the wire.

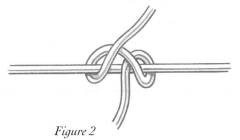

Figure 2

Design: Kristin Fellows and Steven Ford

Sizes: 6-1/2" DIAMETER X 8" (16.5 X 20.5 CM) AND 10" DIAMETER X 7-1/4" (25.5 X 18.5 CM)

5. Thread the beads in place and fasten the other end of the wire to the second ring where you have a spacer. Again wrap the end three times around the ring, cut off the excess, and pinch the end.

6. Working symmetrically—first one side, then the opposite, then halfway between—slip a spacer bead off the wire only as it is replaced by the vertical wire knot. The remaining eight spacers on the second ring are for connecting it to the third ring.

7. Working down the basket, continue making and

connecting rings until you have six in total. If you want to add large beads for "feet," as in the red basket, include sufficient additional spacers in the sixth ring. Don't pierce the beads for the feet completely through; instead, glue the wire ends inside the beads.

8. Make a seventh ring to go inside the sixth to make a bottom. Then, in the center of the seventh ring, create an X with wire and small beads to complete your basket. If you wish, shape the top ring to give it a scalloped appearance.

IKAT COILED VESSELS

USING THE COIL METHOD ALLOWS YOU PLENTY OF LATITUDE TO EXPERIMENT WITH THE SHAPE AND PROPORTIONS OF YOUR FINISHED VESSEL.

■

YOU WILL NEED

About 12 oz. (340 g) of polymer clay per vessel, pasta machine (for ikat pattern), blade, 320-, 400-, and 600-grit wet/dry sandpaper, 0000 steel wool

IKAT CANE PATTERN

1. The pattern shown here, which was accidentally discovered by City Zen Cane, is an imitation of ikat, a traditional weaving technique. To try this, start with two sheets (each rolled on the widest setting of a pasta machine) of contrasting colors. Cut them lengthwise into strips and reassemble the pieces into a single striped sheet.

2. Narrow the setting on the pasta machine and send the sheet through so that the stripes are perpendicular to the rollers. Fold the sheet in half, laying light on light and dark on dark, and send it through again fold first. Do this 10 or 15 times until you have a smooth gradation of tone on the surface of the sheet.

3. On the final pass through the rollers, return to the thickest setting on the pasta machine. Then look at the cross section of the sheet to see the ikat pattern. Double the cross section by adding a second sheet made the same way.

MAKING A COILED VESSEL

1. Begin by forming a long strip of polymer clay. Thin-walled vessels can exploit the qualities of translucent clays to great effect (see the vessel on the cover), but you need a thickness of at least 1/8" (3 mm) for strength. To form the strip, join sections of cane slices or any pattern you choose. If you made the ikat pattern described above, cut strips of the cross-sectional pattern from the flat sheet.

2. Start the base of the vessel by cutting or pinching the strip to a tapered point and coiling it into a small spiral. Tapering the end will give the spiral an even beginning.

3. Continue to coil the strip, placing it edge to edge and pinching together the seams as you go, until you have a disk the size you want for your base. Joining all of the seams (especially with striped strips) is very important for the strength and integrity of the structure.

4. Now begin the walls; slightly pinch up the edges of the base disk and continue coiling. As you build upward, you can control the diameter of the vessel by adjusting the placement of each layer of the coil (figure 1).

5. If your vessel walls are very thin, cut the strip and bake the partially completed piece. Then continue coiling on the baked foundation—after it has cooled—taking extra care to smooth the seam between baked and unbaked clay. For maximum control, you may want to bake every few layers.

6. When it's complete, bake the vessel according to the clay manufacturer's instructions.

7. Wet-sand the outside of the vessel, starting with the coarsest paper and progressing to the finest. Finally, polish it with the finest steel wool.

Figure 1

Design: STEVEN FORD
Size (largest): 2" × 8" (5 × 20.5 CM)

FOOTED PLATTER

RADIANT COLORS AND A CAPRICIOUS DISPLAY OF CANES AND OTHER
DECORATIONS COMBINE TO GIVE THIS FOOTED PLATTER ITS CHARM.

◼

Design: ANGIE WIGGINS
Size: APPROXIMATELY 6" x 5" x 1-1/2" (15 x 12.5 x 1.5 CM)

YOU WILL NEED

About 4-1/2 oz. (127 g) of watermelon-red
and 1 oz. (28 g) of golden yellow polymer
clay, assorted canes, roller, pasta machine
(optional), craft knife, blade, waxed paper,
cheesecloth, coarse sandpaper, curved
armature

MAKING THE PLATTER

1. Flatten the watermelon-red clay into a sheet
about 1/8" (3 mm) thick. (Use the #1 setting on the
pasta machine.)

2. Set the sheet on a piece of waxed paper and outline an abstract shape for your platter. With the
craft knife, cut along the outline. Save the excess
clay for the platter's feet.

3. Using the yellow clay, roll a log long enough to
encircle the platter. After wrapping the log around
the platter, cut off any excess yellow and make a
butt joint.

4. Using the roller, gently flatten the yellow clay so
that it's even with the red. Join the two by smoothing the edges with your fingers. To assist in joining,
place a piece of waxed paper on top of the clay and
smooth the colors with a roller.

5. Decorate the surface of the platter with paper-
thin cane slices, dots of color, and tiny candy canes.
Using a roller over a sheet of waxed paper, smooth
the decorative elements into the platter. Finally, texture the surface by placing cheesecloth onto the
platter and rolling with some force. For a heavier
texture, roll the clay onto a sheet of coarse sandpaper.

6. Carefully lay the platter onto a curved armature
that can withstand the baking temperature; a broad
stone or shallow dish would work well. If the armature is glossy ceramic, metal, or glass, place the
cheesecloth between the platter and armature to
prevent the clay from taking on a shiny finish.

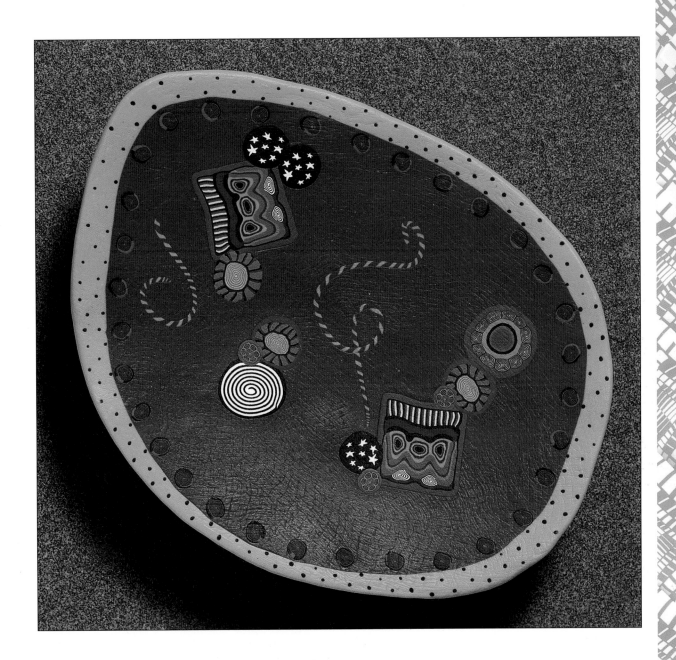

7. For the feet, roll a log about 1/2" (1.5 cm) in diameter from the excess red clay. Cut four pieces 1-1/4" (3 cm) long and decorate them as desired. Press the feet firmly into the center of the bottom of the platter.

8. Bake as directed by the clay manufacturer.

9. Do not remove the platter from the armature until it is cool and be careful not to knock off the feet while the platter is still warm after baking. If one is dislodged, it can be glued in place with cyano-acrylate adhesive.

HEART BOX

PERFECT AS A DECORATION FOR A DRESSER OR BEDSIDE TABLE, YOUR
ONE-OF-A-KIND HEART BOX IS CERTAIN TO BECOME A TREASURED
FAMILY HEIRLOOM.

Design: JAQUI MACMILLAN
Size: 3" x 2-1/2" x 2-1/4" (7.5 x 6.5 x 5.5 CM)

You Will Need

About 12 oz. (340 g) of scrap polymer clay, one or more canes, roller or pasta machine, blade

Making the Box

1. To make the sides of the box, roll a strip of scrap clay about 1/8" (3 mm) thick (or use the #1 setting on a pasta machine) and cut it into a rectangle 8" x 1-3/4" (20.5 x 4.5 cm).

2. Cover the rectangle with very thin cane slices and roll it until the surface is smooth. Then trim the edges to regain the original dimensions.

3. With the cane patterns facing you, stand the rectangle on its edge and fold it into a heart shape (figure 1). Join the edges at the point of the heart and smooth the seam.

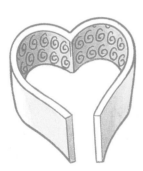

Figure 1

4. Bake according to the clay manufacturer's recommendations.

5. Flatten a second sheet of clay about 1/4" (6 mm) thick for the bottom of the box. Gently press the cooled, baked heart onto the sheet, leaving a mark of its outline. Fill in the marked area with thin cane slices and smooth the surface with your roller.

6. Place the heart back onto the decorated area of the sheet and cut around the outside of the heart, leaving a margin of 1/8" (3 mm) all the way around (figure 2). Smooth this extra clay up the sides of the heart to attach the bottom firmly to the sides.

7. Bake again.

8. The lid for the box is made in two sections. For the outer portion, roll a sheet of clay 1/4" (6 mm) thick. Place the cooled heart on the sheet and cut around it, flush with the sides of the box.

9. The inner portion of the lid is made using a sheet of clay 1/8" (3 mm) thick. Press the baked heart onto the sheet to mark an outline and fill in the marked area with thin cane slices. After smoothing the slices, use the baked heart to cut out the heart shape. This cut will be imperfect and should be trimmed neatly with a blade.

10. Press the two heart-shaped sheets together and smooth the joint (figure 3). Then bake the lid.

11. Now that the basic box is complete, decorate the outside surfaces with cane slices, molded forms, textured bits of clay in contrasting colors, or whatever you desire.

Figure 2

Figure 3

Mary Janes and T-Straps

NOTHING EVOKES CHILDHOOD MEMORIES QUITE SO EFFECTIVELY AS A TINY PAIR OF YOUR FAVORITE STYLE OF SHOES.

Design: MARAH AND DEBORAH ANDERSON
Size: 2-1/4" x 5" (5.5 x 12.5 CM)

YOU WILL NEED

About 4-1/2 oz. (127 g) of polymer clay, pasta machine or roller, blade, aluminum foil, modeling tool, one or more canes, craft knife (T-strap shoes only)

MARY JANES

1. After conditioning the polymer clay and mixing the color you want, roll out two slabs—one for the right shoe and one for the left. Roll the clay about 1/16" (2 mm) thick or use the #4 setting on your pasta machine.

2. Enlarge the patterns in figure 1 by 150 percent and place them on the clay. Then cut out the pieces for the right and left shoes.

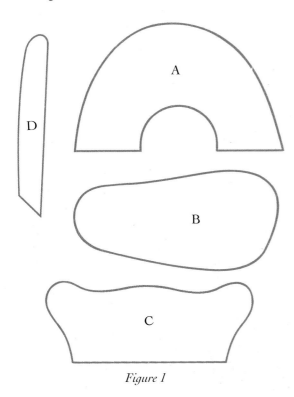

Figure 1

3. Place the toe (A) on top of the sole (B). To hold the two pieces apart, crumple a piece of aluminum foil and place it between the toe and sole. Using a modeling tool, press around the edges to adhere the two pieces, making sure that the foil doesn't creep in between the two layers. Next attach the back (C) onto the heel portion of the sole. After positioning a piece of crumpled foil to hold the back in place, press around the edges to make sure the clay is completely joined.

4. Bake the shoes as directed by the clay manufacturer.

5. After the shoes have cooled, cut several thin slices from your canes and apply them to the shoes. Similarly, decorate the strap (D) with cane slices. Then attach the strap to the shoe. For the button, cut a thick slice from your cane and attach it to the end of the strap.

6. Bake again as directed.

T-STRAP SHOES

1. Using the patterns in figure 2, follow steps 1 and 2, above. Then, using a craft knife, cut out the designs on the toe piece and the buckle.

2. Continue, following steps 3 and 4. After the shoes have cooled, thread the unbaked strap through the slots in the toe piece and into the buckle. You may need to roll the strap a bit thinner to enable it to fit. After attaching the straps and buckles securely to the shoes, bake them again.

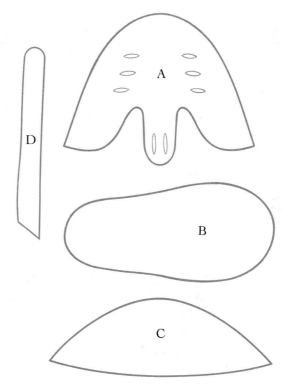

Figure 2

MOSAIC CLOCK

MOSAICS CAN BE CREATED SEVERAL WAYS; WITH THIS METHOD, THE INDIVIDUAL "TILES" ARE PREFIRED TO MAKE THEM EASIER TO ASSEMBLE INTO A COMPLEX PATTERN.

YOU WILL NEED

About 1/2 oz. (14 g) of each of a range of colors, 4-1/2 oz. (127 g) of strong black polymer clay, 2 oz. (57 g) of soft black clay, clock movement, compass or circle template, ruler, paper, pencil, scissors, roller or pasta machine, blade, baking parchment, old credit card or scraper, soft rag, rubbing alcohol, buffing wheel or very fine steel wool

BUILDING A CLOCK FACE

1. Use a compass or template, pencil, and paper to draw intertwined circles, each 1-1/2" (3.8 cm) in diameter, in five rows of five circles. Cut around the outer edge of the drawing to use as a pattern.

2. For the base of the mosaic, it's best to use the strongest polymer clay available. Flatten the strong black clay into a sheet 6-1/2" (16.5 cm) square and 1/8" (3 mm) thick. Then use the paper pattern to cut out the clock base. Cut a hole in the center to accommodate the clock movement.

3. Following the clay manufacturer's guidelines for temperature, bake the base for 10 minutes.

4. Flatten several colors of clay into sheets about 1/16" (2 mm) thick. Place these on baking parchment and cut them into 1/8" (3-mm) squares. For the small, round pieces, make a bull's-eye cane and cut slices 1/16" (2 mm) thick.

5. Bake all of the tiles for about seven minutes at the recommended temperature.

6. After the pieces have cooled, use a roller or the thinnest setting on a pasta machine to roll a paper-thin sheet of soft black clay. Apply the sheet to the base by starting in the center and working the air bubbles out to the edges. Then trim the sheet to match the base and cut a hole in the center for the clock movement.

7. Place the paper pattern onto the clay base and use a dull pencil to trace the circles onto the base. Beginning in one corner, place the tiles snugly onto the base. If necessary, the tiles can be cut with a sharp blade to fit the pattern.

8. When the pattern is complete, bake the piece as instructed by the clay manufacturer.

9. Once the clock has cooled, apply the grout. Roll thin strings of black clay that has been softened to a very pliable consistency and press the clay between tiles with your fingertips. When the entire surface has been grouted, use an old credit card or similar tool to scrape away the excess. Remove the remaining film using a soft rag moistened with alcohol.

10. Bake again as directed.

11. Polish the face of the clock with a buffing wheel or very fine steel wool. Then insert the movement into the hole. A small amount of glue may be required to secure the movement in the hole.

Design: PIERRETTE BROWN ASHCROFT
Size: 6" x 6" (15.2 x 15.2 cm)

Photo Album, Journal, or Scrapbook

Polymer clay makes lovely covers for handmade albums and journals, and you can customize existing hardcover books or binders with your polymer clay designs.

Design: Kathleen Amt
Sizes: 3-1/4" x 4-1/4" (8.5 x 11 cm) and 8-3/4" x 6" (22 x 15 cm)

YOU WILL NEED

Album pages or handmade text pages, two pieces of stiff paper, each cut 1/4" (6 mm) wider and taller than the text pages, polymer clay (see below for determining the amount), roller or pasta machine, blade, spatula, clean scrap paper, "YES" paste (a wheat starch and glycerine compound, available from bookbinding suppliers) or double-sided tape, brush or sponge for applying paste

MAKING A JOURNAL

1. Purchase or make the pages for your journal. An easy way to create your own is to construct an accordion-pleated or zigzag book. Simply fold one long sheet of paper or join several smaller sheets (figure 1). Use paste or double-sided tape to fasten single sheets into a zigzag.

2. To make the covers, you will need enough clay to make two 1/8" (3-mm) slabs, each 1/4" (6 mm) wider and taller than the text pages. One block of clay approximately 2-1/2 oz. (71 g) in weight will make a sheet about 5-1/2" x 5-1/2" x 1/8" (14 x 14 x .3 cm). Because of the heavy usage a book cover may see, choose one of the stronger polymer clays, such as Fimo, Cernit, or Pro-Mat. Additional clay of any variety may be used to decorate the basic covers.

3. Flatten the strong clay into a sheet 1/8" (3 mm) thick. (Use the #1 setting on a pasta machine.) Then use the stiff paper patterns to cut front and back covers. Place each on a sheet of clean scrap paper.

4. Stamp, texture, or decorate the covers. For an overall pattern such as the crackle effect shown on the larger album, make a separate decorative layer. The crackle pattern is made by applying a thin dried-out sheet of clay or a piece of metallic leaf over a thicker slab of soft clay. As the two layers are rolled together, both enlarge and the top layer cracks, exposing the bottom layer. Continue rolling the two until the decorative layer is about 1/16" (2 mm) thick; then trim it to size.

5. Press the decorative layer onto the base cover using a roller. To minimize trapped air pockets, roll from the center out to the edges. Place the paper pattern on top and trim the cover to size as needed.

6. Remove the scrap paper backing by inverting the slab onto another sheet of paper and gently pulling the paper back at a sharp angle. Try not to bend the cover as you do this. Then place both covers face up and bake them according to the manufacturer's instructions.

7. While they're still hot, remove the covers from the baking tray with a spatula and place them between two clean sheets of paper. Press them under some books or other heavy weight until they're cool.

8. Finish the journal by attaching the pages to the covers. One approach that works well with an accordion-pleated book is to glue the first page to the inside of the front cover and the last page to the inside of the back cover. If you have a collection of single pages, an easy method for binding them into your covers is to drill holes along one side of the covers and the text and insert decorative rings, ribbons, or laces into the holes.

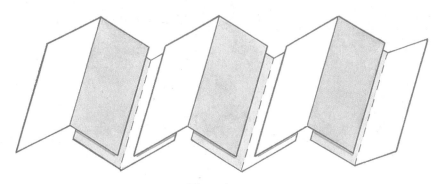

Figure 1

Drapery Rod Ends

CUSTOMIZED DRAPERY RODS ADD THE PERFECT FINISHING TOUCH TO A
CAREFULLY DESIGNED ROOM.

Design: SARAH SHRIVER
Size: APPROXIMATELY 2-1/4" (5.5 CM) DIAMETER

YOU WILL NEED

Pair of wooden knobs 2-1/4" (5.5 cm) in diameter (to fit a 1-1/2" or 4-cm rod), less than 2 oz. (57 g) of polymer clay, roller or pasta machine, cutting blade, one or more canes, small brass heishi, small black glass beads, brass head pins, electric drill, cyanoacrylate glue

MAKING THE KNOBS

1. Begin by covering the ball part of the knob. It is important to get the solid covering of polymer clay to lie snugly against the wooden knob because if there are any air pockets, they will expand during baking. Flatten the clay into a sheet about 1/16" (2 mm) thick and cut a skirt-shaped piece (figure 1) to cover one quarter of the ball. Position it so that the small curve fits tightly around the narrowest point between the ball and the flared base, and the large curve is at the widest part of the ball (figure 2). Try not to stretch the clay to fit; instead, let it lie naturally and trim it with a blade.

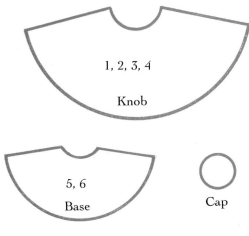

Figure 1

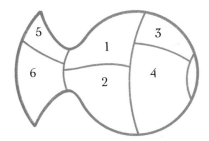

Figure 2

2. Cut another skirt of clay to complete the cover for the inside half of the ball. This piece should be slightly larger than needed so that it can be cut to fit precisely. When applying this piece, begin at one edge of the first piece; then wrap it around until it overlaps the second edge. Press lightly on the overlap, making a registration mark, and cut along the marked line. Smooth both seams gently; then trim the line around the diameter to make it even.

3. Cut and fit the third and fourth pieces as you did the first two. When applying the third and fourth pieces, place them so that the seam isn't in line with the seam between the first two pieces. Trim the open circle at the cap and cut a piece of clay to fit.

4. Screw the knob into something solid so that it stays vertical; then bake it as directed by the clay manufacturer.

5. Once baked, you can handle the ball part of the knob while covering the base. Cut the same basic shapes, but make more extreme angles for the base pieces than for those that covered the ball. Apply them one at a time, smoothing the seams and trimming off any excess clay around the edge of the base.

6. Bake again.

7. The end of each of these rods is decorated with a large cane slice. A band of clay, repeatedly incised with the end of a pen cap, encircles the cane slice. Ten small, contrasting triangles decorate the base, and a band of incised clay covers the seam between the ball and base. Small cane slices dot the remainder of the knob. Once you're finished adding decorations, bake again.

8. To add beads, drill tiny holes through the centers of the small cane slices and at the tips of the triangles. Cut head pins to fit the holes. Then add a bead to each pin, coat the pins with glue, and insert them into the holes.

MOSAIC-PATTERNED TIN

ORDINARY STORAGE TINS MAKE BEAUTIFUL DECORATIVE CONTAINERS
WHEN EMBELLISHED WITH YOUR FAVORITE POLYMER CLAY DESIGNS.

■

YOU WILL NEED

About 4-1/2 oz. (127 g) each of white and purple polymer clay, 2-1/2 oz. (71 g) each of orange, green, and brown clay, roller, pasta machine (optional but recommended), blade, clean scrap paper, ruler, tin container or other object, 120-, 200-, 400-, and 600-grit wet/dry sandpaper, medium and fine steel wool, wax or mineral oil

MOSAIC CANE

1. A mosaic cane is constructed using numerous square logs—one for each square of color in the pattern. One of the two patterns included in this tin has 11 rows of 11 logs, and the other has 15 rows of 15 logs. Using colored pencils and graph paper, it's easy to devise your own patterns.

2. Begin by making uniform slabs of each color. Use the #1 setting on a pasta machine or flatten each to a thickness of 1/8" (3 mm). Then cut each slab into a rectangle.

3. To assemble your cane, cut 1/8"-wide (3-mm) strips from the various slabs (figure 1) and place them on a piece of clean paper. Assembling the cane on a piece of paper will allow you to move it more easily later. When placing the strips, lift them with your blade to prevent distortion. Set each strip firmly alongside the preceding one, allowing no gaps between them.

Figure 2

Figure 3

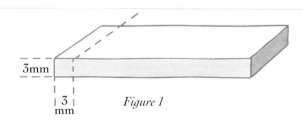

Figure 1

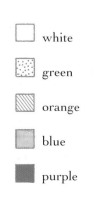

white

green

orange

blue

purple

4. Create your pattern row by row, starting with the bottom layer. Figures 2 and 3 show the two patterns used here. When the pattern is complete, your cane

Design: MICHELE FANNER
Size: APPROXIMATELY 3" x 3" x 4" (7.5 x 7.5 x 10 CM)

MOSAIC-PATTERNED TIN

■

should be square with no lumps or hollows. Using your roller, smooth the cane on all sides and square the corners. Reduce the cane to the desired size by continually turning and rolling, taking care not to distort the pattern.

COVERING THE TIN

1. After measuring the box and lid, flatten a paper-thin sheet of dark green clay. (Use the #5 setting on a pasta machine.) Cut one piece large enough to wrap around the sides of the tin and cut a second piece to cover the lid.

2. Wrap the sheet around the tin, pressing it in place so that air bubbles don't become trapped between the clay and the metal sides (figure 4). Trim the end and smooth the joint. Then press the other sheet onto the lid. If you detect any air pockets after you have applied your base layer, prick them with a needle or your blade to release the air; then gently smooth the surface with your fingers.

3. Now cut very thin slices from the mosaic cane(s) and apply them to the sides and lid of the box. This tin uses four slices in each row and four rows for each side (eight slices of each cane).

4. If your cane slices don't meet at the corners, use decorative slices or solid-colored logs to fill the gap. On this tin, small purple logs make colorful accents and neatly finish the edges.

5. Make a small purple cone for the "handle" on the lid. This is baked separately and glued to the tin later.

6. Bake the tin and cone as directed by the clay manufacturer.

7. After baking, glue the cone onto the front of the lid. Then wet-sand all surfaces well, starting with the coarsest paper and finishing with the finest. Polish the sanded surface with medium, then fine steel wool and apply a thin coating of wax or mineral oil.

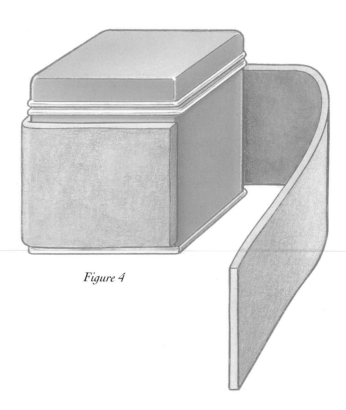

Figure 4

PICTURE FRAMES

CUSTOM-CRAFTED PICTURE FRAMES MAKE IDEAL GIFTS, AND THEY'RE A SNAP TO DO IF YOU START WITH AN INEXPENSIVE WOOD OR METAL FRAME.

YOU WILL NEED

Geometric pattern: about 2-1/2 oz. (71 g) each of blue, white, and black polymer clay

Leopard skin pattern: about 1 oz. (28 g) of brown, 1/2 oz. (14 g) each of beige and black polymer clay, 250-grit wet/dry sandpaper

Mokume-gane pattern: About 8 oz. (226 g) of translucent, 1/2 oz. (14 g) of peach-colored polymer clay, four sheets of metallic leaf, tracing or waxed paper, large darning needle

All patterns: roller or pasta machine, blade, wood or metal frame

GEOMETRIC CANE

1. Using black clay, roll a long log about the thickness of your little finger and shape it into a triangle. Wrap this with a thin sheet of white, a thin sheet of black, and a thick sheet of blue clay.

2. Next, make a block of black and white stripes using four thick sheets of white and four thin sheets of black. Cut three to four 1/8"-thick (3-mm) slices from the striped block. Then join the slices end to end and wrap them around the cane so that the stripes run lengthwise (figure 1).

CIRCULAR FRAME BY ROSANNE EBNER

3. Finish by wrapping a thin layer of black, then a thin layer of blue clay around the entire cane.

4. Reduce the cane to an appropriate size for your frame and apply slices directly onto the metal or wood.

5. Make another cane to fit into the negative spaces. Bull's eyes, spirals, or solid colors accent the negative spaces nicely.

6. To finish the frame, place slices of a striped cane around the inside edges of the frame. Make the striped cane by using a thin sheet of black on both sides of a thick sheet of blue and alternate that combination with a thick sheet of white.

7. Bake the frame according to the clay manufacturer's recommendations.

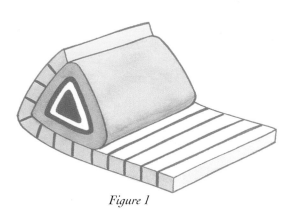

Figure 1

PICTURE FRAMES

■

LEOPARD SKIN CANE

1. Using the brown clay, roll out a log the thickness of your thumb. With your fingers, gently press around the log to give it an uneven, irregular surface (figure 2).

2. Place irregularly shaped strips of black polymer clay around the log, leaving some small sections of the log uncovered (figure 3). Then wrap the entire log with a thin sheet of beige clay.

3. Cut the log into six equal segments and arrange the pieces into a group with one piece in the center and five others around it. Gently roll this until the pieces fuse into one cane.

4. After reducing the cane to the diameter of your little finger, cut it into four equal pieces. Combine the four segments and reduce the cane once more.

5. Again cut the cane into four equal pieces and reassemble them. Roll the cane to fuse the pieces together. The cane is now complete.

6. Apply slices of the cane directly to the frame, smoothing the edges where the slices join each other.

7. To make a perfectly smooth surface, wet-sand the finished piece after it has been baked.

MOKUME-GANE

1. Using the translucent clay, make five cubes in progressively larger sizes from 1" (2.5 cm) to 2-1/2" (6.5 cm). Blend a pea-sized portion of peach clay with each cube to get a progression of pastel shades.

2. Roll each cube into a flat sheet a little more than 1/16" (2 mm) thick. (Use the #3 setting on the pasta machine.) Try to make the sheets about the same size and shape as your metallic leaf.

3. Place your lightest colored sheet of clay on the tracing or waxed paper and cover it with one sheet of metallic leaf. Working slowly, continue layering by alternating sheets of progressively darker clay with sheets of leaf. When finished layering, trim the edges of your loaf with the blade.

4. Roll small pieces of the peach clay into balls of various sizes—none exceeding a large pea—and push them into the darkest layer of clay. The placement and size of the balls will determine the final pattern.

5. Now turn over the loaf so that the darkest layer is on the bottom. Starting in the center and moving outward, gently press down on the loaf between the balls so that you are distorting it to form small hills and valleys. If the loaf is soft after all of this manipulation, let it cool and stiffen overnight.

6. Prepare the frame by applying a thin layer of translucent clay to it. Noting the lower temperature generally required for translucent clay, bake the frame.

Figure 2

Figure 3

Designs: ROSANNE EBNER (BLUE GEOMETRIC),
TERRI RUBENSTEIN (LEOPARD SKIN),
ROBIN WRIGHT (METALLIC MOKUME-GANE)
Sizes (left to right): 7-3/4" x 5-3/4" (19.5 x 14.5 CM), 3" (7.5 CM)
DIAMETER, 6" x 8" (15 x 20.5 CM), 2-1/2" x 3-1/2" (6.5 x 9 CM)

7. With your blade, cut thin slices horizontally off the top face of the hills on the loaf. Set these aside. Once the pattern is sufficiently revealed, begin cutting paper-thin slices of uniform thickness and layer these onto the frame until it is completely covered. Press the slices together, filling any gaps with the scraps set aside earlier.

8. Merge the edges with a roller; then use the darning needle to apply a ridged surface that resembles gathered cloth. Tip: The more structured the textural pattern is, the more difficult it is to maintain.

9. Carefully bake the frame, making sure that it doesn't darken.

CANDLESTICKS

PART OF THE APPEAL OF THESE DRAMATIC CANDLESTICKS COMES
FROM THE FACT THAT EACH IS SLIGHTLY DIFFERENT, WHILE ALL SHARE
THE SAME COLOR SCHEME.

■

YOU WILL NEED

About 6 oz. (170 g) of polymer clay per candlestick, 2"-diameter (50-mm) metal washer, fiberglass-reinforced tubing 6-8" (15-20 cm) long and 3/8" (1 cm) in diameter, copper plumbing pipe cap, electric drill, head pins, cyanoacrylate glue, small decorative beads (purchased or your own)

BUILDING THE COMPONENTS

1. To make the base, form a ball of scrap polymer clay about 1-1/2" (4 cm) in diameter and cover it with a very thin layer of solid-colored clay or a mosaic of cane slices.

2. Center the ball on a heavy metal washer, pressing down to cover the washer and create a mound shape about 1" (2.5 cm) high. The washer will be visible on the bottom; use it as a design element or cover it with clay as desired.

3. Using scrap clay, make a second ball somewhat smaller than the first. This will become the decorative element midway up the stem, so decorate it accordingly.

4. Arrow shaft tubing, a fiberglass-reinforced material, makes an effective stem because it is light and strong, and the clay adheres well to it. A wooden dowel can be substituted, but the clay won't adhere as well. Cover the tubing with a thin sheet of clay, making a butt joint and smoothing the seam carefully.

5. A candle, copper pipe cap, or mold of an existing candle holder can be used to form the candle cup. Cut a circle of clay 1/4" (6 mm) thick, using your form to establish the diameter. From a sheet at least 1/8" (3 mm) thick, cut a strip of clay 1/2-3/4" (1.5-2 cm) wide and bend it around your form to make a cylinder. (Apply some talcum powder on the form to make it release easily.)

6. Without removing the form, make a butt joint and smooth the seam of the clay cylinder. Then attach the circle of clay to the bottom edge of the cylinder, carefully smoothing the seam. While the cup is still supported by the form, decorate it however you choose. You can also shape the candle cup or give it a zigzag top edge, but you must maintain enough thickness and height to support a candle.

7. After removing the form from the candle cup, bake all of the components as instructed by the clay manufacturer.

ASSEMBLY

1. Measure the outside dimension of your stem; then mark the center of the other three pieces with a circle slightly smaller than the size of the stem. In the base, drill a hole about 3/4" (2 cm) deep. Drill all the way through the decorative ball; then drill into the bottom of the candle cup without drilling through it.

2. Slide the decorative ball onto the stem and anchor it in place with rings of clay around the top and bottom. Place the bottom of the stem into the base and use another ring of clay to hold the two pieces together and hide the seam. If the stem wobbles in the base, fill any gaps with clay to secure it. Fill the top of the stem with a pea-sized ball of clay before placing the cap on the stem; then secure the cap with another ring of clay.

3. Add more decoration—textures, cane slices, and the like—and bake the candlestick as directed.

4. After baking, drill several tiny holes down into the center of the candle cup through the pea of clay that was added. Into these holes, apply head pins coated with a couple of drops of glue. These provide some extra reinforcement to the union of the candle cup and stem.

5. Add finishing touches by drilling holes in various parts of the candlestick. Thread beads onto head pins that have been cut slightly longer than the depth of the holes; then apply glue to the pins and insert them into the holes. Press until the beads are flush against the surface of the clay.

Design: SARAH SHRIVER
Sizes: 7-1/4" (18.5 CM), 5-1/4" (13.5 CM), AND 6-1/2" (16.5 CM) TALL

MIRRORS

THE FRAMES FOR THESE FANCIFUL MIRRORS ARE MADE ENTIRELY OF
POLYMER CLAY, AND THIS APPROACH ALLOWS YOU TO CUT THE MIRROR
ANY SIZE AND SHAPE YOU WISH.

■

Design: BRIDGET ALBANO
Sizes: 8" x 12" (20.5 x 30.5 CM), 14" x 6-1/2"
(35.5 x 16.5 CM), 7" x 9" (18 x 23 CM)

YOU WILL NEED

One 12"-square (30.5-cm) mirror tile, glass-cutting tool and lubricant, about 3-1/2 oz. (99 g) of strong polymer clay, roller or pasta machine, blade, assortment of canes or other designs (totaling about 6-8 oz./170-226 g), sheet of rag paper, medium-grit sandpaper, 20-gauge wire, round-nose and needle-nose pliers

CREATING THE MIRRORS

1. Lubricate the glass-cutting tool and cut the mirror tile into three pieces as shown in figure 1. With warm soapy water, wash off the lubricant from the mirrors, taking care not to cut yourself on the sharp edges.

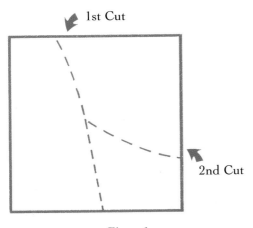

Figure 1

2. Flatten the strong clay into a sheet about 1/8" (3 mm) thick (or use the #1 setting on a pasta machine) and cut several 1"-wide (2.5-cm) strips. On your baking surface, arrange the strips into the shape of one mirror. After joining the pieces together, lay your mirror on top so that you have about 1/4" (6 mm) of clay showing all around.

3. Decorate the front of the mirror by applying the designs one at a time and pressing them onto the overlapping clay from the back. Each design on these mirrors has a small pad of clay underneath it to add dimension to the frame.

4. Bake as instructed by the manufacturer; then allow the mirror to cool.

5. Set a sheet of rag paper on your baking sheet and place the mirror with the front side facing down onto the paper. (This will prevent shiny areas.) Lightly sand the clay on the back of the mirror and add another thin layer of strong clay for reinforcement.

6. Using the round-nose pliers, make two loops with short pieces of wire. Crimp the ends of the wire into a zigzag with needle-nose pliers (figure 2). Press the loops into the reinforcing clay, placing them about 2" to 3" (5 to 7.5 cm) from the top of the mirror. Then cover the zigzag ends with a thick mound of strong clay.

7. Bake as directed.

8. When the clay is cool, connect the two loops with a piece of wire (figure 3), and your mirror is ready to hang.

Figure 2

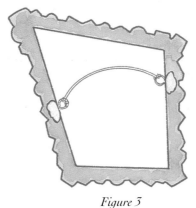

Figure 3

FLORAL NAPKIN RINGS

STYLIZED YET NATURAL IN APPEARANCE, THESE FLORAL NAPKIN RINGS
WILL ADD A TOUCH OF SPRING TO YOUR TABLE.

■

Design: DONNA ESHER
Size: APPROXIMATELY 3-1/2" (9 CM) DIAMETER

YOU WILL NEED

About 2-1/2 oz. (71 g) each of leaf green, white, and pale yellow polymer clay, roller or pasta machine, craft knife, live leaves with prominent veins, assortment of teardrop-shaped cutters (optional)

MODELING A RING AND FLOWER

1. For each ring, make a "stem" of green clay that is long enough to encircle a napkin. Form the stem into a circle and smooth the joint with your finger. The size of your ring will determine how large you should make your flower.

2. Roll the balance of the green clay into a sheet a bit less than 1/8" (3 mm) thick or run it through the pasta machine on the #2 setting. Use a craft knife to cut two or three 2"-long (5-cm) leaves per napkin ring and smooth the cut edges to round them slightly. To make veins, press the clay leaves onto a real leaf or incise a vein pattern into the clay using a pointed tool.

3. For the petals, use a craft knife again or the teardrop-shaped cutters. Cut one large petal for a calla lily, one small and two medium petals for an orchid, or four small and five medium petals for a rose. For the orchid, add a vein pattern in the small petal as you did with the leaves.

4. Make a stamen by rolling a thin finger of pale yellow clay and tapering one end into a rounded point. For a more realistic look, gently roll the stamen over a textured surface. (The handles on some craft knives have perfect textures for this.)

5. Place the finger of clay on the lower end (the full, round part, not the point) of the appropriate petal and gently wrap the lower edges of the petal over the stamen to close the bottom of the flower. To complete the orchid, add two more petals. Curve and bend the petals to give them a natural appearance.

6. To make a rose, roll one small petal into a spiral that is tight in the center and fairly loose around the outside. Add three small petals, gently wrapping them around the central bud. Now add five medium petals around the outside of the flower.

7. Complete the flower by adding two or three leaves behind it. Curve the base of each leaf to the base of the flower to adhere the clay together. Then arrange the flower on the ring so that it lies perpendicular to the ring.

8. To prevent the napkin rings from deforming while baking, place them on a wooden dowel or cardboard tube. Make sure to anchor the ends of the dowel or tube to your baking pan. Then bake the pieces according to the clay manufacturer's instructions.

DOMINOES

THE DESIGN OF THESE MERRY DOMINOES IS A DARING DEPARTURE
FROM THE TRADITIONAL PATTERN OF WHITE SPOTS ON BLACK.

■

YOU WILL NEED

About 11 oz. (311 g) of polymer clay,
several different cane designs, roller,
blade, incising tool or one blank domino

ABOUT THE GAME

A standard set of dominoes contains 28 pieces, or
"bones," each about 3/4" x 1-1/2" x 1/4" (2 x 4 x .6
cm). One side of each tile has an engraved design,
and the other is divided into two equal squares, each
with the pattern of one face of a die. The set consists
of all possible combinations (21 in total) that can
occur by rolling two dice, and the blank is added to
provide seven more combinations.

MAKING THE PIECES

1. Roll a thick slab of polymer clay and cut 28 rectangular tiles approximately the size of actual dominoes. Adjust the size to please your hand and eye,
but make all of the rectangles as uniform in size as
possible. Then round the corners and smooth the
edges to make them pleasant to handle.

2. Stamp or incise a design on the back of each soft
polymer clay tile. In this set, the artist used the back
of an actual domino to imprint the traditional
insignia.

3. On the opposite face of each tile, draw two
squares to divide the surface in half. This is easiest if
you stamp it with a blank domino (a tile without any
dots) to impress an outline of the two square halves
onto the soft polymer.

4. To give a visual divider between the two squares,
place a thin, narrow slice from a colorful cane across
the center line of each tile.

5. Make a variety of eye, mouth, and nose canes in
different colors, sizes, and expressions. You will
need six different faces to substitute for dice patterns. Using thin slices from the canes, arrange the
faces in every combination of two per tile, placing
them forehead to forehead. For the final seven
dominoes, position a face on only one end of each of
six tiles and leave one domino completely blank.

6. Smooth all of the cane slices firmly in place and
bake the dominoes according to the clay manufacturer's recommendations.

Design: LIZ MITCHELL
Size (each): 3/4" x 1-1/2" x 1/4" (2 x 4 x .6 CM)

BACKGAMMON

ADD A TOUCH OF CLASS TO YOUR WEEKEND GAMES OF BACK-
GAMMON WITH A CUSTOM SET MADE OF "MARBLE" AND "JADE."

Design: SUSAN KINNEY
Size: 7" x 12" x 1" (18 x 30.5 x 2.5 CM)

YOU WILL NEED

About 4-1/2 oz. (127 g) each of black, white, and translucent polymer clay, scant amounts of light green, orange, and purple polymer clay, blade, food processor (recommended but not required), blade, roller or pasta machine, ruler, 7" x 12" (18 x 30.5 cm) sheet of cardboard, extra pieces of cardboard, cyanoacrylate glue (optional), black acrylic paint, small artists' brush

CONSTRUCTING THE BOARD AND PIECES

1. To make the black marble, begin by chopping about one-eighth of the white clay into chunks about 1/8" to 1/4" (3 to 6 mm) in diameter. Use a food processor if one is available. Then chop all but about 1 oz. (28 g) of the black clay. After setting a few crumbs of black aside to use later in the faux jade, sift the balance of the chopped clay together with the white chunks.

2. Roll this into a log and twist it to produce a streaking effect. If you want more white streaks, add more white chips; then roll and twist again. When the marbled pattern looks satisfactory, flatten the clay into a sheet about 1/4" (6 mm) thick.

3. Cut the sheet into a rectangle 5" x 14" (12.5 x 35.5 cm). Then cut two strips 1" x 12" (2.5 x 30.5 cm) for the sides, two strips 1" x 5-1/2" (2.5 x 14 cm) for the bottom middle piece of the board, and two strips 1" x 7" (2.5 x 18 cm) for the ends.

4. Flatten a second sheet and cut 24 triangles, each 3/4" (2 cm) wide at the base and 3" (7.5 cm) tall. This is easiest if you first cut a triangle pattern from the extra cardboard.

5. For the "white marble," chop the remainder of the black clay as above. Then chop a small amount of translucent clay. Finally, chop the remaining white clay and sift in the chips of black and translucent. Roll and twist the colors together until you have a marbled effect you like.

6. Roll the white marble into sheets about 1/4" (6 mm) thick and cut 12 triangles identical in size to the black ones. Cut two strips 1" x 7" (2.5 x 18 cm) to stack and place in the center of the board.

7. Make 15 white marble game pieces by rolling 1/2" (1.3-cm) balls and flattening them into wafers. After flattening, the pieces should be no wider than 3/4" (2 cm) to fit on the triangles.

8. Begin the "jade" by conditioning three-quarters of the leftover translucent clay and mixing in a 1/3" (8-mm) ball of green clay. Divide the remainder of translucent in half; then mix a 1/8" (3-mm) ball of purple into one portion and a 1/8" (3-mm) ball of orange into the other. Chop each tinted portion separately and mix them into the pale green clay by twisting and rolling the colors together. Add the tiny crumbs of black and twist again until you are pleased with the result.

9. Roll this into a 1/4" (6-mm) sheet and make 12 triangles as before. Form 15 game pieces that are the same size as those made from the white marble. Then make three cubes about 3/4" (2 cm) on each side. Incise the dot pattern of regular dice onto two of these and incise the third one with the numerals 2, 4, 8, 16, 32, and 64.

10. Using the cardboard rectangle as a base, assemble the board one half at a time. Alternate the three colors of triangles along the outer edges of the cardboard, as shown in the photograph, and place one of the black marble strips lengthwise in the center. Roll the surface gently to bind the pieces together and smooth the edges.

11. Then place the double-layered white marble strip across the middle of the board, trimming it enough to accommodate the sides of the board. Repeat the assembly process for the other half of the board.

12. To attach the sides and ends, you can either bake the pieces separately and glue them onto the board later, or you can press them onto the board now and brace them with cardboard while baking.

13. Bake the board and all components as directed by the polymer clay manufacturer.

14. After the pieces have cooled, tint the dots and numerals on the dice with the black acrylic paint.

CHRISTMAS TREE ORNAMENTS

HOLIDAY ORNAMENTS THAT ARE DECORATED WITH YOUR PERSONAL
CANE FAVORITES WILL BECOME CHERISHED ADDITIONS TO YOUR TREE.

ORNAMENT BY MARY MCWILLIS-BRENTANO

YOU WILL NEED

Glass ornament, one or more canes, latex
gloves, blade, ornament hanger, 200-, 400-,
and 600-grit wet/dry sandpaper, 0000 steel
wool, vegetable oil or wax or water-based
matte finish, toothpick, cyanoacrylate glue

COVERING THE ORNAMENT

1. Remove the metal cap from the top of the ornament and set it aside.

2. Cut slices about 1/8" (3 mm) thick from your
canes and apply them directly to the ornament. It
doesn't matter where you start—one artist begins at
the neck and the other at the bottom of the ornament. Place the slices so that the edges touch and fill
any gaps with slices from smaller canes. Resist the
urge to press the slices in place; a glass ornament
breaks easily when pressure is applied, and the clay
slices will stick to each other and hold securely.

3. When the ornament is fully covered, put on a pair
of latex gloves and *gently* roll the ornament in your
hands as if you were making a huge bead. (The
gloves will prevent fingerprints.) As your hands
warm the clay, the cane slices will expand and fill in
the ridges and depressions. The smoother you can
make the ornament at this step, the easier the final
sanding will be.

4. Carefully replace the ornament cap and attach the
hanger. Suspend the ornament over a deep dish and
bake as directed by the clay manufacturer.

5. For a very smooth surface, wet-sand the ornament, progressing from the coarsest paper to the
finest. Sand very gently to avoid sanding through
the clay. Then polish the surface with steel wool.

6. Finish the piece with oil or wax, or apply a commercial matte finish according to the manufacturer's
instructions.

7. Using a toothpick, place a small amount of adhesive where the cap meets the neck of the ornament.
Allow the glue to dry before hanging the ornament.

Designs: MARAH AND DEBORAH ANDERSON (RED BELL, DARK BLUE, LIGHT BLUE, AND BONE SPHERES) AND
MARY McWILLIS-BRENTANO (GREEN AND RED SPHERES)
Size: APPROXIMATELY 2-1/2" (6.5 CM) DIAMETER

DECORATED EGGS

PETER CARL FABERGÉ WASN'T THE ONLY ONE TO APPRECIATE THE PERFECT FORM OF AN EGG; WHEN COVERED WITH SLICES FROM YOUR FAVORITE CANES, A COLLECTION OF DURABLE EGGS MAKES A MAGNIFICENT YEAR-ROUND DECORATION.

YOU WILL NEED

One or more uncooked, fresh chicken or goose eggs, piercing tool, thin knitting needle or skewer, absorbent cloth, one or more canes, blade, roller or pasta machine, screwdriver or similar tool, 320-, 400-, and 600-grit wet/dry sandpaper, 0000 steel wool, heavy rags or paper towels

PREPARING THE EGG

1. Carefully pierce the egg by making a small hole in the center of each end with your piercing tool. Break up the yolk by lightly poking the tool around inside the egg; then blow out the contents.

2. Pour or blow warm water into the egg, shake well, and blow out again until the water is clear. Then set the egg with one hole facing down on absorbent cloth and leave it for a few days to dry out completely or pop it into a warm oven.

3. Cane slices can be applied directly to the egg, or a thin layer of polymer clay can be baked on to give the shell a second skin to make it stronger. An easy way to add a uniform layer to an egg is to apply one or two strips of clay around the middle and fit a circle of clay on each end. Pierce the clay through the original holes in the egg. Then skewer the egg as if it were a large bead, suspend it over a pan, and bake.

CRAZY QUILT EGGS

1. Canes with small repeat patterns that resemble fabric work best for this design. Cut about 20 slices—three or four from each different cane—and make them all the same thickness by putting them through a pasta machine or by rolling them to an even thickness of about 1/8" (3 mm). Then cut about five or six of the slices into polygons that vary in shape and size (figure 1).

2. As you work, hold the egg in one hand, placing your thumb and middle finger over the holes. Starting with your largest prepared slice, lay it near the center of the egg and press down gently to adhere it to the surface. Take another, contrasting slice and place it so that it abuts the first one. *Don't* smooth the seam between the slices.

3. Keep adding slices, cutting different shapes as needed to fill the gaps. As you work, take care to keep from touching the slices already placed on the egg; the warmth of your fingers will soften the edges of the slices and make them look sloppy. Cover the entire egg except the two spaces under your fingers; leave these until after you have added the "stitches."

4. If you need to set the egg down while you prepare more slices, gently lay it on a smooth surface to avoid marking the clay.

5. Using any tool that leaves a thin mark—a small screwdriver, metal ruler, etc.—make small impressions at regular intervals along every seam to give the appearance of stitches.

6. Let the egg sit for a while to cool and harden the slices. Then cut and place the final slices over the ends and add stitching to the seams. For best results, place two slices over each hole so that the seam crosses the hole. During baking, this allows

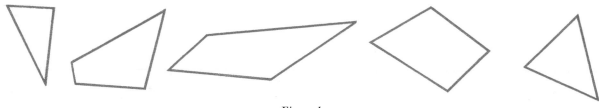

Figure 1

Designs: SUSAN PADGITT SCHWAB (ROSES, CATS, COUGAR), LAURA OAKES (CRAZY QUILT), AND STEVEN FORD AND DAVID FORLANO (MOSAICS, GEOMETRIC TUBULAR PATTERNS)
Sizes: APPROXIMATELY 2" x 2-1/2" (5 x 6.5 CM) AND 2-1/2" x 3-1/2" (6.5 x 9 CM)

air to escape through the tiny gap in the seam and prevents bubbles from forming in the clay.

(If you want to smooth the seams together and cover the holes completely, bake the egg by bringing up the temperature from a cold oven. When the egg has finished, take it out and check to see if the clay has bubbled out over the holes. If so, gently press it flat with an oven mitt while the clay is still warm.)

8. Suspend the egg over a pan in the oven and bake it according to the clay manufacturer's recommendations.

SMOOTHLY POLISHED EGGS

1. To polish a decorated egg to a smooth finish, wet-sand it by hand, using first the coarsest, then progressively finer grades of wet/dry sandpaper. If desired, finish with steel wool to increase the luster. To avoid making flat spots, turn the egg continually in your hand as you sand it.

2. For a shine that looks natural, buff the egg vigorously with a substantial rag (denim is good) or a heavy-duty paper towel. It helps to reheat the egg in a warm oven before buffing, since this will soften the clay and speed up the process. A fine coating of furniture wax produces a nice sheen.

CHESS SET

IT'S ESPECIALLY FUN TO PLAY CHESS WHEN THE PIECES HAVE CHARACTER; EACH PIECE CAN BE UNIQUE, BUT REMEMBER TO MAKE ONE SET LIGHT IN COLOR AND THE OTHER DARK.

■

YOU WILL NEED

About 1-3 oz. (28-85 g) of polymer clay per piece, assortment of canes, blade, inexpensive set of chess pieces for models, coarse sandpaper, acrylic paints, rag, 00 steel wool

SCULPTING THE PIECES

1. Establish the relative size and general shape of your chess pieces by using the existing set as a model. Make all of the pieces from solid polymer clay to give them some weight and character. The most economical use of your material is to make the basic form using scrap clay and apply a decorative veneer of cane slices or other patterns.

2. Make each piece using a combination of simple forms. For example, the queen has seven components joined together: three wafers of different thicknesses, two cylindrical shapes, one teardrop, and a crown.

BUILDING A ROOK BRICK BY BRICK

1. The rook shown is constructed like a brick building, using 59 individually cut blocks. Begin by mixing walnut-sized balls of clay in four or five dark red/brown colors. Flatten the balls and cut small, brick-shaped blocks.

2. Press the outer surface of each block onto a piece of sandpaper to add texture. Don't worry about the surface looking too rough; it will be smoothed later.

3. Assemble the bricks, trimming and pinching them into wedge shapes to accommodate the shrinking diameter as you work from bottom to top. To give the piece an overall modulation in tone, vary the colors as you place the bricks.

4. If you find it difficult to build a tall structure in one operation, try constructing it half way, baking, then completing the structure once the baked foundation has cooled.

5. Following the clay manufacturer's guidelines, bake the completed rook.

6. Enhance the worn look of the surface of the piece by adding an acrylic patina. (The queen also has a gray patina that accentuates the surface qualities of the clay.) Mix a grayish brown in acrylic paint and work a small amount into all of the cracks, gaps, and surface irregularities. Before it dries, rub most of the paint off the surface, first with a rag and then with steel wool. The result is a weathered, battered look that is worthy of a fortress.

Design: STEVEN FORD
Sizes: FROM 2" (5 CM) TO 4" (10 CM) TALL

BIRD HOUSES

THESE DELIGHTFUL BIRD HOUSES ARE AS PRACTICAL AS THEY ARE DEC-
ORATIVE; A PLASTIC LID ON THE BOTTOM OF EACH ONE ALLOWS YOU
TO CLEAN HOUSE BETWEEN TENANTS.

YOU WILL NEED

Empty coffee can with plastic lid to fit,
heavyweight paper plate, 24-gauge wire,
wood perch, about 9 oz. (255 g) of polymer
clay, tin snips, metal punch or nail, ham-
mer, needle-nose pliers, stapler

CONSTRUCTING THE BIRD HOUSE

1. Using the punch and tin snips, make a small
round opening for the bird on one side of the can.
Make it slightly larger than you need, since you will
cover the edges with a layer of polymer clay.

2. Mark the center of the paper plate and cut a line
from the center to the edge. Now form the plate into
a cone, placing it onto the can to adjust the height of
the roof. When the shape of the roof is satisfactory,
staple it together well.

3. Punch two small holes side by side in the center
of the top (closed) end of the can. Then loop the
wire through the holes and thread the ends up
through the center of the roof (figure 1). Pull the
roof tightly onto the can and finish with a loop at
the top.

4. Temporarily place the plastic lid onto the bottom
(open) end of the can. This will prevent you from
accidentally covering the bottom edge with clay.
Just remember to remove it before baking.

5. Using solid colors of clay or canes from other
projects, cover about one-third of the can at a time;
then bake. This will prevent you from damaging the
surfaces previously applied. Add the perch last,
using a thick ball of clay to hold it securely.

6. Now cover the roof with a thin layer of clay,
adding texture if you wish. Cover it to the bottom
edge; then bake. When it is cool, hold the can
upside down and cover the edges and underside of
the roof. Fill in the V-shaped area between the
house and roof so that the two are firmly attached.
Then decorate the roof as desired and bake again.

7. If you want to use your bird house outdoors,
apply a thick coat of neutral shoe wax and buff it dry.
Rainwater seeps into the plastic lid on the bottom and
causes rust around the metal lip. To minimize this,
periodically coat this area with wax as well.

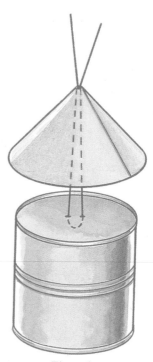

Figure 1

Design: BRIDGET ALBANO
Size: 4-1/4" DIAMETER X 6-3/4" (11 X 17 CM)

NATIONAL POLYMER CLAY GUILD

The National Polymer Clay Guild is an independent, nonprofit organization that is dedicated to educating the public about the use of polymer clay as an artistic medium. Although it is based in the Washington, DC, area, the Guild has more than one thousand members who represent every state plus eleven foreign countries.

The Guild publishes an excellent newsletter, *POLYinforMER*, which contains tips and techniques, new information and research, and lists of classes, workshops, and meetings of polymer clay groups working around the United States. The Guild has an extensive slide bank and lending library of books related to polymer clay. It also sponsors gallery shows of members' work and promotes polymer clay as a serious medium to museums. Once a year, members have the opportunity to get together for a long weekend to demonstrate techniques and exchange ideas at an annual retreat.

The Guild is a terrific resource for connecting with other polymer clay artists and staying on top of the latest information about polymer clay crafts. For more information about joining, write to The National Polymer Clay Guild, 1350 Beverly Road, Suite 115-345, McLean, VA, 22101.

ONLINE WITH POLYMER CLAY

If you want to ask questions and share ideas about polymer clay, it no longer matters where you live. With a computer and modem you can dial into an entire community of fellow aficionados. Commercial services (such as America Online, GEnie, Prodigy, and Compuserve) have groups that you'll find helpful; they're generally listed under arts, crafts, jewelry, or beads. On the Internet, you can dial into a newsgroup called rec.crafts.polymer-clay.

If you're new at cruising the 'net, spend some time reading messages and learning the etiquette before posting your questions. Don't be surprised if you feel lost on your first few tries. There are lists of Frequently Asked Questions (FAQ), which may contain just the information you need. There are also lists of suppliers that have been compiled by artists from around the world.

Online friendships can become surprisingly strong, and fellow artists often pull each other out of slumps and temporary crises. Where else but at your fingertips can you find so much shared enthusiasm for your chosen craft?

TREE BY VIRGINIA SPERRY, APPROX. 8-1/4" x 4-1/2" (21 x 11.5 CM)

Allen, Jamey D. "Millefiori Polyform Techniques." *Ornament* 12 (Summer 1989): 46-49.

Carlson, Maureen. *FIMO Folk.* Canby, OR: Hot Off the Press, 1992.

Cuadra, Cynthia. "Master Class with Tory Hughes: Polymer Clay Simulations." *Ornament* 17 (Winter 1993): 84-91.

——. "Master Class with Tory Hughes: Polymer Clay Simulations, Ivory and Turquoise." *Ornament* 17 (Spring 1994): 84-89.

Dierks, Leslie. *Creative Clay Jewelry.* Asheville, North Carolina: Lark Books, 1994.

Dubin, Lois Sherr. *The History of Beads.* New York: Abrams, 1987.

Dustin, Kathleen. "The Use of Polyform in Bead-Making." *Ornament* 11 (Spring 1988): 16-19.

Eberhard Faber. *FIMO Ideas for Creative Modelling.* Neumarkt, Germany: Eberhard Faber, 1988.

——. *New FIMO Modelling Ideas.* Neumarkt, Germany: Eberhard Faber, 1986.

Edwards, David. *Using FIMO.* San Diego: David Edwards, 1990.

Francis, Peter, Jr. *Beads of the World.* Atglen, PA: Schiffer, 1994.

Gessert-Tschakert, Evelyn. *Modelling Fashionable Jewelry with FIMO.* Neumarkt, Germany: Eberhard Faber, 1987.

Harris, Elizabeth. *A Bead Primer.* Prescott, AZ: The Bead Museum, 1987.

Haunani, Lindly. "Mokume Gane." *Bead & Button* 7 (February 1995): 20-22.

Hjort, Barbara. "Buttons and Beads: Bake Your Own from Polymer Clay." *Threads* 39 (February/March 1992): 58-61.

Jensen, Gay. "Discover Polymer Clay." *Shuttle Spindle & Dyepot* 22 (Winter 1990-91): 46-49.

Luters, Ginger. "Clay Play." *Bead & Button* 1 (February 1994): 16-18.

Mattson, Jo Ann. "Friendly Faces." *Bead & Button* 2 (April 1994): 11-14.

National Polymer Clay Guild. *POLYinforMER* (newsletter published five times per year, started in January 1991). McLean, VA.

——. *Polytips and Tidbits: Resources.* McLean, VA: National Polymer Clay Guild, 1993.

——. *Polytips and Tidbits: Techniques.* McLean, VA: National Polymer Clay Guild, 1993.

Oroyan, Susanna. *Fantastic Figures.* Lafayette, CA: C&T, 1994.

Roche, Nan. "Creating with Polymer." *Shuttle Spindle & Dyepot* 22 (Winter 1990-91): 52-53.

——. *The New Clay.* Rockville, MD: Flower Valley Press, 1991.

Ross, Anne L. "City Zen Cane." *Ornament* 15 (Winter 1991): 70-71, 87.

——. "Master Class with City Zen Cane: Polymer Clay Ikat Technique." *Ornament* 18 (Spring 1995): 74–79.

Rufener, Shirley. *Fancy FIMO Jewelry.* Canby, OR: Hot Off the Press, 1992.

Toops, Cynthia. "People Beads." *Bead & Button* 6 (December 1994): 13-17.

CONTRIBUTING ARTISTS

Bridget Albano
Claymont, DE
Pages 5, 108, and 123

Kathleen Amt
Mt. Ranier, MD
Pages 25, 55, 77, and 96

Deborah and Marah Anderson
San Jose, CA
Pages 92 and 117

Pierrette Brown Ashcroft
Accokeek, MD
Pages 4 and 95

Laura Balombini
Blue Hill, ME
Page 22

Thessaly Barnett
Oakland, CA
Page 44

Mary McWillis-Brentano
Portland, OR
Pages 116 and 117

Claire Laties Davis
Edgewood, RI
Pages 27 and 53

Kathleen Dustin
Bellaire, TX
Pages 3, 12, 13, and 53

Rosanne Ebner
Merrick, NY
Pages 103 and 105

Donna Esher
Ventnor, NJ
Pages 110 and 111

Michele Fanner
Wanniassa, Australia
Pages 24 and 101

Kristin Fellows
Rose Valley, PA
Page 85

Steven Ford and David Forlano
Philadelphia, PA
Pages 5, 6, 9, 14, 15, 37, 56, 72, 85, 87, 119, and 121

Ruth Anne and Michael Grove
Berkeley, CA
Page 17

Lindly Haunani
Bethesda, MD
Page 44

Sarajane Helm
Escondido, CA
Page 52

Tory Hughes
Berkeley, CA
Pages 32, 33, 42, and 54

JoAnne Hunot
Santa Barbara, CA
Pages 7, 8, 34, 41, 49, and 57

Marie Johannes
Birmingham, MI
Pages 10 and 46

Donna Kato
Chicago, IL
Pages 8, 47, and 51

Susan Kinney
Asheville, NC
Page 114

Karyn Kozak
Chicago, IL
Page 23

Z Kripke
La Jolla, CA
Pages 41 and 78

Marguerite Kuhl
Melbourne, FL
Page 45

Tamela Wells Laity
Weaverville, NC
Pages 19 and 71

Sarah Lee
Ann Arbor, MI
Page 18

Liz Mack
Bloomfield Hills, MI
Pages 26, 48, 49, and 63

Jaqui MacMillan
Washington, DC
Page 90

Liz Mitchell
Pittstown, NJ
Pages 22 and 113

Laura Oakes
Duncanville, TX
Page 119

Susanna Oroyan
Eugene, OR
Page 20

Susan Perry and Bill Gundling
Guttenberg, NJ
Page 57

Carolyn Potter
Pasadena, CA
Pages 10, 30, 42, and 80

Cheri Pyles
Ketchikan, AK
Pages 8 and 63

Anna Riddile
Houston, TX
Pages 45, 82, and 83

Nan Roche
College Park, MD
Page 43

Terri Rubenstein
Baldwin, NY
Page 105

Maggie Rudy
Portland, OR
Pages 21 and 47

Susan Padgitt Schwab
Davie, FL
Page 119

Sarah Shriver
San Rafael, CA
Pages 98 and 107

Alan Slesinger
New York, NY
Page 24

Wilcke Smith
Albuquerque, NM
Pages 16 and 45

ACKNOWLDGMENTS

Special thanks to Richard Babb and Kathleen Holmes, without whom this book would not be nearly so rich a feast for the eyes, and to David Forlano for his flexibility and support. Thanks also to Cynthia Tinapple for her assistance with online resources, to Cynthia McIlwain for her time spent on behalf of a good friend, to Nan Roche, Kathy Amt, Kathleen Dustin, Pier Voulkos, and Tory Hughes for all of their ideas and helpful information, to JoAnne Hunot for providing an assortment of colorful letters, and to WNC Ceramic Tile of Asheville, North Carolina for generously lending us props.

Linda Soberman
Huntington Woods, MI
Page 43

Virginia Sperry
Ellicott City, MD
Page 124

Lynne Sward
Virginia Beach, VA
Page 44

Sam Terry and Dave Allender
Sunnyvale, CA
Page 57

Cynthia Toops
Santa Fe, NM
Pages 10 and 31

Pier Voulkos
Oakland, CA
Pages 9, 28, 29, and 50

Angie Wiggins
Powhatan, VA
Pages 5, 88, and 89

Elise Winters
Haworth, NJ
Pages 73 and 74

Robin Wright
Forest Lake, MN
Page 105

INDEX